Purposetivity

*The Feminine Face of Productivity
for Time, Team & Tech*

Karen Fritz

Purposetivity: The Feminine Face of
Productivity for Time, Team, and Tech
by Karen Fritz

Cover Design by Colleen Davis
Copyright © 2017 by Karen Fritz

ISBN: 978-1-944177-51-5 (p)
ISBN: 978-1-944177-52-2 (e)

Crescendo Publishing, LLC
300 Carlsbad Village Drive
Ste. 108A, #443
Carlsbad, California 92008-2999

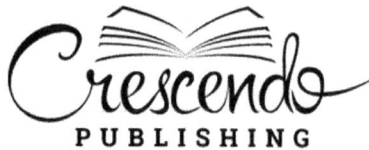

Crescendo
PUBLISHING

Message from the Author

Click the video link to hear a personal message from Karen Fritz, author of Purposetivity.

https://youtu.be/xnftazePJTE

I'm so delighted you've stepped up to discover your customized us all. I want you to be able to unleash your full attention to what way to integrate your personal and professional activities from your soul's intention. Bringing your gift to the world is urgent for matters most!

You can get started right now by discovering your Purposetivity Persona – your purpose - driven productivity and leadership strengths and opportunities – with this free assessment! *See precisely where you stand with the Time, Team and Tech crucial to scaling your business.*
http://PurposeDrivenProcess.com/purposetivity_persona

I really want you to get the most out of this journey, in the easiest possible way! So I've created a set of business plan template notebooks for you to use in Evernote to capture your research and ideas as you go.

Just go to http://www.PurposeDrivenProcess.com/bptemplates to download your template as well as a complete set of worksheets to accompany this book!

Dedication

To my sons, Kyle and Connor, and to Youth of Unity—the next generation who accepted me into their circle and let me see the dreams, inclusiveness, and passionate courage coming next to the marketplace. May this transitional time create a world ready for the innovation and meaning you bring to it.

Table of Contents

Introduction

"What will you do with your one wild and precious life?"
~ Mary Oliver

What do you do when that thing that you are known for goes away? When that thing that keeps you safe, that makes you valuable in the world vanishes? Whether it's your beauty or your strength, your helpfulness or your knowledge, when that thing you trade on to keep you going is gone?

For me, it was sudden, and it was invisible.

Growing up, I was smart. Hella smart. "Gifted" they'd call it now. Early in elementary school I helped the teacher grade papers, which made me pretty unpopular with my classmates but did get me in out of the cold during recess (so I couldn't be bullied anyway). Being smart kept me warm and safe.

Smarts got me grades. Grades got me scholarships. Scholarships got me university education. University grades got me a good job. I had my choice of job offers, and I chose the one with the culture for excellence, where I could learn and achieve and change the world.

Of course, not all my coworkers saw it that way. They literally had someone come ask me to tone down the achievement because I was making them look bad. I missed out on the popular thing again.

In fact, that particular corporate culture changed, as did most of them, and I jumped at the chance to take a severance package in 1991. I supported (and then some) the family with various entrepreneurial ventures. Whether learning totally new fields or consulting back to corporate, I've loved the freedom and independence. Being an entrepreneur enabled me to go as fast and as far as I wanted, for the sheer joy of learning and achieving. I never looked back.

I was blessed with a "mind like a steel trap"—all knowledge, appointments, pending actions were instantly accessible. Spelling, locations of kids' toys, husband's keys ... right there.

Early in 2013, I lost it.

My memory ... wasn't there.

My words ... weren't there.

No one else could see. The deficit was totally invisible (especially if I stayed home).

Menopause hit me hard. Not only the lack of estrogen to the brain centers for language and memory, but weeks on end of hemorrhaging that led to anemia. During that year, I addressed health challenges with every means I could find. The following year, I stabilized more or less by sleeping—fifteen or more hours every day, with frequent rests between. I managed to publish *The Art of Adventure* in 2014, but I couldn't really get out there and make anything from it.

The following year, I started regaining some stamina but still "had no words." The brilliantly articulate communicator had vanished. The muse was gone. And without my verbal-processing bridge, I had no short-term memory, which translated to no long-term memory. My health was improving slowly, but my business practice was in shambles.

Poking around the web for something to interest me, I happened on Steve Dotto's "Evernote Made Easy" webinar. Evernote - salvation and heaven in one! A place I could take notes on all the things I should be remembering—and have them with me on my phone at the store! A place I could gather thoughts to create again! A tool to collect all the random notes and documents of ideas that I had splattered over my computers! I couldn't wait to share it with my motorcycle touring buddies as a way to help in trip planning and organizing ride reports! (I know, there are a lot of exclamation points in that paragraph. It felt so good to be interested in something again!)

Only a month later my coaching mentor bemoaned being so overwhelmed with internet marketing details that she had no time to expand her body of work. That just seemed so wrong! So I told her I'd come over on Saturday and we'd get things figured out. I had no idea what would transpire; I just knew I was supposed to be there.

As I sat on the floor with colored pens and flip-chart paper, I asked her all about what she loved and hated and wanted for her business and life. In developing technical training, I'd learned to receive information in random order based on interviewing a dozen different software developers, so I just wrote it all down. Then I started doing what I did for software: I diagramed how the pieces fit together.

That paper filled with circles and arrows was a turning point. My mentor saw it as transformational. It gave her clarity on what she was building and where the next missing piece was. I thought it was nothing—until I realized that the two *perspectives* spoke volumes to our different styles. I tend to be a geek: task first, relationship second; balanced between right and left brain; a logical, systems view with a creative and charismatic flair. My much adored mentor is a visionary who loves to connect deeply with people: an excellent businesswoman with a thriving practice, systems and details come second to her.

My huge aha: **I am here to support, empower, activate, and launch people who are *not* just like me!**

I see the future trending toward relationships and collaboration. The difference of bringing heart to our marketplace is long overdue! I want every heart-centered businesswoman out there connecting and giving her gift. Personally, though, I'm an introvert who really prefers her quiet office. I love to give a dynamite talk loaded with value—yay! Then I go home and cocoon to recharge. A paradox to be certain, but I'm not going to fight it. What I DO want to do is bring my gift to the service of others.

So here we are.

Section 1
Purpose and Plan

Chapter 1
Purposetivity:
On-Purpose Activity

Purposetivity gives you a set of perspectives to look at and **align your soul's intention, heart's desire, head's plans, and hands' work**.

You don't need another way to bulldoze your way through fragmented tasks or to bully yourself to do distasteful things. Quit trying to fake yourself out. **Every action you take can be sourced in something deeper**, tied to gratitude that you *have* things that matter to you!

Shifting our fundamental relationship to time and score keeping, and redefining success as experiencing fulfillment rather than achievement or accumulation, give us a qualitative alignment in every aspect of our daily business and life.

Purposetivity is about becoming more fully embodied as our soul contributing in this world, making us **more deeply human in the most divine way**. Your soul's intention flows outward to create your personality's true nature. From those, you choose *what* to change in the world and then *how* to engage with that in alignment with who you truly are.

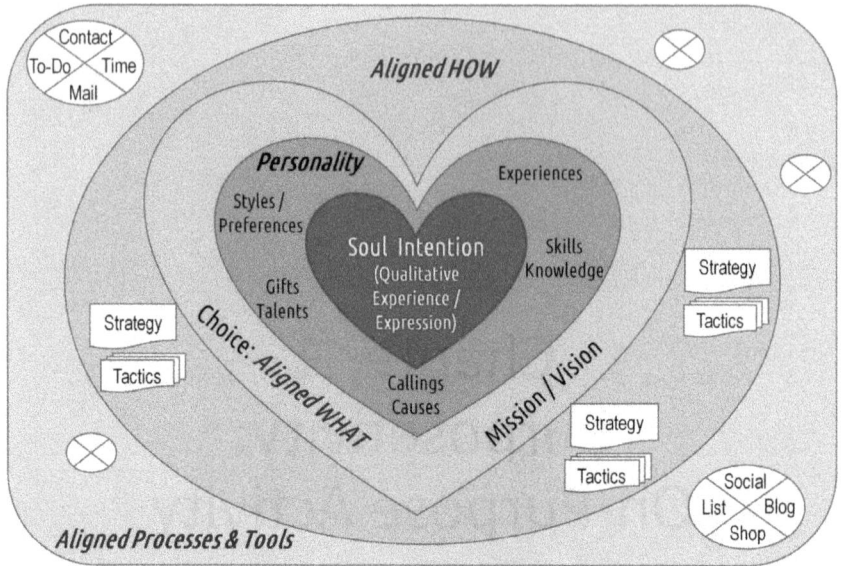

When meaningful fulfillment (in accordance with our unique expression) is the direction, our perspective on time shifts naturally. No longer the enemy, wherein we have to do all the "musts" and meet all the expectations before we earn the right to participate in fulfilling activities, **time becomes the inner experience of our moment-to-moment quality of flow**. It becomes the medium for our journey, the conduit or vehicle.

Purposetivity is a conscious approach to time, communication, and action in the context of our true self, dreams, and diversity. This book will show you how to look at your plans with a new lens, choose your strategies and tactics with new criteria, implement the new things with integrity, and review it all with gratitude.

Why Does This Shift Matter? Discovering the Active Feminine

We have a slight misconception in our society (imagine that!) that the masculine is the part of us that goes "outward," that reaches for goals, is active in the world, and achieves. Somehow "some of us" have taken the penis as the ultimate expression of effectiveness— be rigid, shove your way in, take relentless action toward a single goal. Starts to sound pretty silly, doesn't it?

Meanwhile the feminine culturally has a limited role as "receiving" in a more passive way, nurturing what is already within the fold and holding space. In the best of cases, the feminine is seen as the creative source of ideas, which must then be pursued from our masculine side. But fundamentally, the old social ideology of "feminine" is helpless, weak, passive, ineffectual. Impotent. And you know as well as I do that's sure as hell not true!

You know, not all cultures see things this way! A more common global perspective has the masculine holding protective space while the feminine gestates and births the new creation. The feminine is the movement of creative power while the masculine is power in stillness.

So when I say that Purposetivity is the "feminine face of productivity," I mean it is also about taking positive action in the world, simply not the linear, brute force, overriding forms that have been used in the field. **With a feminine face, we see action sourced from a deep place of creative power, gathering in the heart and supported by the mind, always connected, one fabric of intention-desire-plan-action.**

Ending the days of production-line or cubicle "professionalism," we no longer need to wear masks of emotionless, disconnected mind-bots. Living a whole life by **bringing all of who we are to everything we do**, we no longer need to compartmentalize or look for some mythical "balance." It's all HERE. Right here. Right now. All.

For too long, a few industrial visionaries (barons) have mapped out the experience of a multitude of workers. As we become more informed and self-referential, the old ways don't fit. They were designed and promoted for a purpose by a specific subset of society—linear males optimizing profit—in their image.

Too many creatives over the years (decades, centuries) have contorted themselves into time management and productivity systems perfectly UNsuited for them. And their personal gift was crushed, drowned out in the process.

If linear, left-brain, regimented systems don't work for you, maybe **it's not your fault or failing.**

Maybe it's just time for some **creative reinvention** of how to relate to time *your way*. Because you matter and your gift is unique.

Purposetivity's integrated approach to creating a business and lifestyle that are both fulfilling and financially sustainable makes a difference on three levels: personal, professional, and for the planet.

On the personal level, designing everything from strategy to tools to fit who you really are enables you to *feel* confident that you have a handle on all the pieces. You get the satisfaction of clear, effective action without second-guessing yourself all the time. You'll find you waste less time and energy spinning, avoiding (think Facebook, TV, retail therapy), or just glorifying busyness. Rather than lamenting the (not-so) subtle shame of ADD, you can exploit your multi-passionate nature with an approach to work within your lifestyle that actually feels good! **You can love all the people and passions that you love** and let them ride the rhythm of waves of attention.

On the professional level, you have more capacity to dream beyond dollars; in addition to financial rewards, what experience of fulfillment are you creating? When you're not frittering your time and attention away on trivial filler tasks, you get to reclaim your competency and power as a creative person. You'll find when you align your *way of engaging*, you actually **make more progress on what's most important** to you. You get the results that really matter. With an overarching vision, you know how all the pieces and activities contribute so that you don't get distracted by "shiny bright objects" (SBOs) or suffer from "fear of missing out" (FOMO). You have clarity in your direction and the courage to meet unavoidable challenges with grace.

And for our society and planet, as we step into more authentic, enjoyable ways of integrating business and personal activities, I see the emergence of more tolerance – even celebration – of others' unique purposes, styles, and roles. By recognizing and engaging the diverse gifts we each bring, **we shift the commercial realm (at least) to mutual support and compassion**. This is why bringing out the feminine face is so crucial! When our soul gifts actually get to come out into the world, we see the sustainable innovation that brings more Life for all.

Chapter 2
The Purpose of Life

"The purpose of life is to discover your gift.
The work of life is to develop it.
The meaning of life is to give your gift away."

~ David Viscott

For us to be able to work from the inside out in this book, we'll need a shared context for purpose and meaning. When I talk about the soul's intention, I'm referring to an aspect of the Divine that has individuated in order to create a quality of experience.

Soul Intention
(Qualitative
Experience /
Expression)

Our soul's purpose is something far more nuanced than completing a task or achieving an outcome. It has a subtle "texture," a quality of engagement with Life as a whole. **Business is the perfect vehicle to challenge us to show up in our truth**—to discover, clarify, and express our unique signature of qualities and energies.

When we discern our signature qualities and align our activities to experience and express them more, we feel fulfilled, and we get to uplevel and experience more depth and breadth of aliveness. Not every business owner needs to build an empire and "play big." It may be that **without any element of hiding, she can "play deep" in a very focused game and give her gift most fully**.

Much of our growth journey in business revolves around finding innovative ways to express our unique gifts visibly in a culture traditionally steeped in masks and positioning.

Do we dare to be seen for who we really are?
Do we dare withhold it any longer?

How Do I Know?

While we may not be consciously aware of the qualities and energies our soul is working with, they've always been active in our lives. Sometimes we can recognize them by themes of what we've experienced; sometimes by themes of experiences that were lacking. Journaling can provide insights, yet it's a dicey proposition to "hear" the language of the soul beneath the manufactured certainties of the ego's training.

An excellent process for articulating the qualities of experience your soul wants to experience and express through your personality is knowing your Divine Coordinates®.

Through my Divine Coordinates, I know my soul's intention is to "activate your unique expression of the Divine through intimacy and transformation." My expression of that showed up in how I raised my sons and it shows up in every chapter of this book. Another way I sometimes say it is, "I am creative power in motion, cherishing and embracing higher expression."

A certified Divine Navigation Coach (like me!) can guide you through a fully lucid conversation that dips below your intellect to identify true resonance in your deepest self. Knowing those energetic qualities, your coach becomes your partner in observing what's active in your life and how to bring more engagement with fulfilling activities. You can find out more at: www.DivineNavigtion.com.

Danielle LaPorte's book *The Desire Map* provides a more do-it-yourself, lighter-weight process. Using meditation and journaling to tap into the *Core Desired Feelings* you want throughout your daily activities, you create guiding words for your goals.

As I went through her process, I was able to articulate that I want to feel "creative, inspired, passionate, and joyful," so I keep those in mind when I'm comparing possible business strategies. Which one allows me to feel the way I want to feel?

A third system deeply rooted in soul qualities is the Enneagram. Originally sourced in mystical traditions, the Enneagram provides insights into personality traits and driving motivations.

Conscious Expression

*"Are you a good witch
or a bad witch?"*

~ Glinda in The Wizard of Oz

In whatever way you dive below the surface to discover keys to your soul's intentions, coming back to daily life bumps right into rules you've been taught, norms you've absorbed, and the image you have of yourself within those.

Learning your soul's direction is your entry point. Now your workout becomes recognizing when it contradicts your habits—that whole (not so) comfort zone you've created and maintained with all your might. Now you get to see it for the limiting cage it has become as you have grown.

The ruthless self-honesty called for in Purposetivity builds your muscles in turning your keys to freedom, alignment, and harmony so that you can open that cage door wide.

Chapter 3
The Purpose of Business

The Purpose of Business and the Purpose of YOUR Business

Consider a model of business that looks at low-to-high profits and low-to-high fulfillment.

If you are having fun but your business doesn't make any money, it's a hobby. And hobbies are great—we should all have many of them! We just need to be honest about what we're up to.

If you make no money and hate what you're doing, you're defeated before you start.

On the other extreme, if you make a lot of money but feel unhappy, you're on the highway to burnout.

What we're looking for in our entrepreneurial ventures is sustainable success, in both finance and fulfillment!

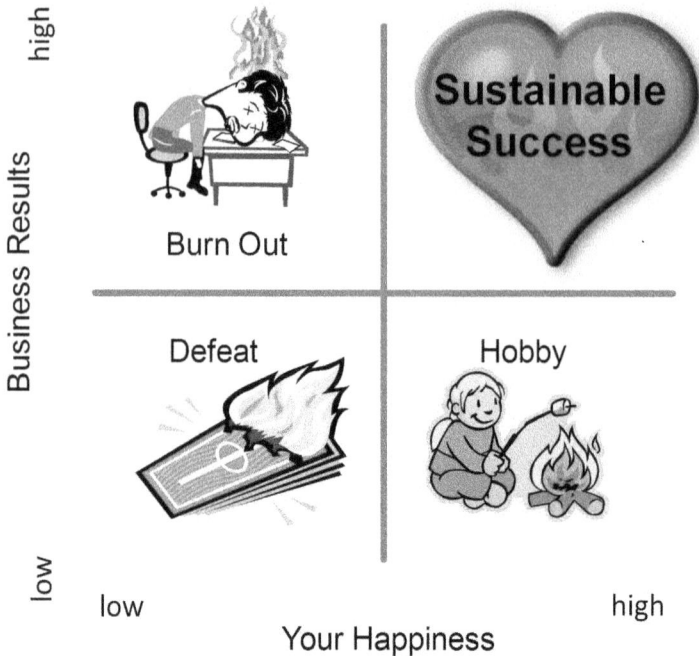

Business Results

low

Burn Out

Sustainable Success

Defeat

Hobby

low   Your Happiness   high

Idolizing Profit

So how does our postmodern culture come up with this concept that business equals profit above anything else?

Adam Smith's 1790 model of economics had **two** elements:

1. People create businesses to pursue their personal self-interest.

   Educational institutions could model this mathematically as money and made it the ONLY basis.

2. People naturally desire and need to care for others and for ideals that transcend self.

   According to Smith this is the *more powerful* aspect of human nature, but it was **disregarded in theoretical oversimplification**.

By 1970, the famous economist Milton Friedman taught simply that the purpose of business is maximizing profit for the shareholders.

Into 1993, management consultant Peter Drucker still focused on profit, even if indirectly. He wrote that the purpose of business is to create and keep a customer *because* the purpose of every business is to create revenues that emanate from the customer.

You Are Not Alone in Reclaiming Fullness

Thoughts started shifting visibly in 1994 when John Elkington wrote about the triple-bottom-line accounting framework for measuring results in "People, Planet, Profit."

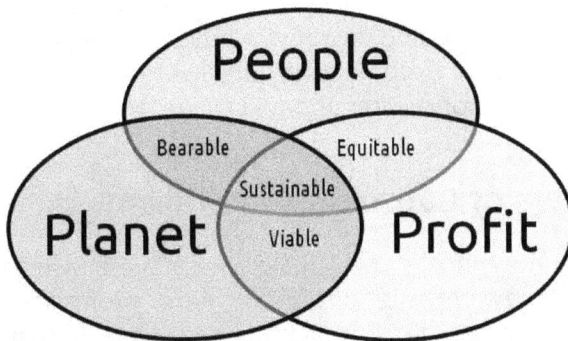

New models emerged as analysts noticed surprising results from companies like Southwest Airlines, Costco, and Trader Joe's, as documented in 2003, *Firms of Endearment* by Raj Sisioda. By 2013, *Conscious Capitalism* by John Mackey, CEO of Whole Foods Market and Raj Sisioda, expressed this clearly: **"The purpose of business is to create sustainable value for all stakeholders."** These leaders have a sense of being called upon to seek the common good, to make a difference, to make the world a better place for their having been there.

In 2010, benefit corporation (B-Corp) legislation began paving the way to cross over between not-for-profit and investment-based structures. The purpose of a benefit corporation includes creating general public benefit, which is defined as a material positive impact on society and the environment. A benefit corporation's directors and officers are **required to consider the impact of their decisions not only on shareholders but also on society and the environment**. By 2015, thirty states authorized B-Corps structures, and B Lab provided certification globally. Certified organizations voluntarily meet certain standards of transparency, accountability, sustainability, and performance, with an **aim to create value for society**, not just for traditional stakeholders such as the shareholders. The movement's motto is "**Business as a force for good.**"

But what about the bottom line? Fully engaged corporations **outperformed the S&P 500 Index by a factor of 10.5** between the years of 1996 and 2011. According to Tony Schwartz, "Companies that Practice 'Conscious Capitalism' Perform 10x Better," [Harvard Business Review, 2013]. This creates a win-win-win because vendors and team members work with the company rather than creating a tug-of-war, and customers buy into the purpose as well as the products and become more loyal. As he says in the article, "The inescapable conclusion: it pays to care, widely and deeply."

Four Pillars of Conscious Capitalism

Many of us now in our own businesses have had experience in traditional large companies or offices where "professionalism" and image-making ruled our interactions. We were indoctrinated to leave emotions at the door along with any of our "personal issues." We learned that so long as we were on the clock, we represented The Company and must exclusively promote and protect The Company's interests. Much of economy 1.0 (Industrial Age) and 2.0 (Information Age) based its interests on exploitation—of environmental resources, of human capital, and of consumers.

What I want to tell you is that while those dinosaurs and business models are in the ugly throes of extinction, the new **ways are already emerging**! You are in the forefront, and you are not all alone!

One of the movements is Conscious Capitalism, which has businesses large and small all over the globe and chapters in many cities where you can connect with like-minded leaders and share best practices. In addition to Whole Foods, consider Patagonia, Southwest Airlines, Costco, and The Container Store, among many others.

Based on the book by the same name, Conscious Capitalism provides four simple perspectives or pillars on which your business can base shared and sustainable success.

The First Pillar: "Shared Purpose"

By openly stating your mission and values, in addition to sustainable profits, you create a higher sense of purpose that engages your customers, team members, vendors, and community to share their creativity and commitment with you.

The Second Pillar: "Stakeholder Orientation"

Certainly your business creates profits, whether you have external investors or a closely held solo venture. From the perspective of Stakeholder Orientation, though, shareholders and owners are not the *only* beneficiaries—perhaps not even the most important. Your other stakeholders include team members, customers, the community, philanthropy, vendors, and even competitors, **all interdependent in your business ecosystem**.

The Third Pillar: "Conscious Leadership"

Your leadership looks to create value for all stakeholders through co-creative win-win-win solutions. **Money is ONE measure of value, but certainly not the only measure**. To actively look for synergy and to be open to multiple kinds of value—such as visibility for vendors, empowerment for team members, trust for customers, and transparency for management—you need a systems perspective, an inclusive way of thinking about business.

The Fourth Pillar: "Conscious Culture"

Engaging stakeholders openly in the purpose and values of your business builds consistency and commitment that holds through times of transition. By making your values public, team members self-select in (or out of) your organization based on match, and customer loyalty goes far beyond price shopping.

Cultures can vary quite a bit, but they usually share traits such as empowerment, growth, transparency, integrity, even love. This inclusiveness and flow from depth to action are **hallmarks of the feminine principle in action**. Staying in that relational space of attention to the whole and adapting as needed is a big part of how these companies outperform old-school corporations.

Business: Infuse Our Life with Meaning

Each of these four perspectives probably already makes sense to you, and you can find ways to **incorporate them into your business more intentionally right now**. You don't need some infusion of venture capital or high-end IT department.

Conscious Capitalism is one approach to "craft a purposeful life while earning a living." This level of **making business matter** is already in your reach, and this book is about steps to proceed to do just that!

"Imagine a business that exists in a virtuous cycle of multifaceted value creation generating social, intellectual, emotional, spiritual, cultural, physical, and ecological wealth and well-being for everyone it touches while also delivering superior financial results year after year." ~ John Mackey

Why do I include all of this? To let you know you are NOT alone! The movement has already begun!

"The secret of change is to
focus all of your energy,
not on fighting the old,
but on building the new."

~ Socrates

Chapter 4
Compare Lifestyle Business with "How Can I IPO?"

In the wild times of the dot-com era, the start-up venture's focus was to innovate something "disruptive," get it to market, make a killing on it, and have an exit strategy ready: sell the company to a big corporation or sell stock in an IPO. Grab your cash with both hands and head off to the next roulette table.

Michael Gerber pretty much defined "entrepreneur" in his 1990 book *The E-Myth* (and later *E-Myth Revisited* in 2004). The philosophy is that you invent a widget and desire to maximize profits, so you learn to "think like an entrepreneur" and learn all the business mechanics so that you can IPO (or the business runs itself without your involvement).

But I don't think coaches (counselors, therapists, healers, and professionals) always *want* that. I think we want to outsource their business mechanics **so that we can focus on the craft we love**, focus on giving from our hearts and making our difference in the world. For transformational messengers, it's not about widgets and exit strategies.

Even those transformational messengers who build multiple income streams in highly visible empires enjoy getting back to the roots of what they really love.

How do we reimagine process and strategy from the craftsman's perspective?

Redefining Progress: Cycles, Seasons, and Phases

Success can no longer be universally defined as continuous growth as measured by market share or revenue. In a purpose-driven business, success equals deepening fulfillment, according to our soul's desires, in a wholistic perspective of uplifting experience for all stakeholders.

The tools and strategies that come along with the old entrepreneurial model don't work because **the goal isn't the same.** The entrepreneurial model has a built-in assumption that the only definition of progress/success is endless growth: bigger, better, more, faster. But for the craftsman, it's about depth. Quality. Intimacy. Even love.

So processes and strategies that are built to support a continuous linear progression fit like the wrong size shoe. Squeezing here, rubbing there—generally just a pain.

Continuous growth doesn't reflect reality. It doesn't reflect the natural world.

The sun does not rise, then keep rising and rising forever.

The summer does not come, then continue to get "more summer" forever.

The moon does not wax, then continue to grow and grow until it takes over the sky.

And women, with our moon cycles, understand this. We live it.

Here we have an alternate basis for developing business strategies and processes that reflect a natural approach.

Just as we experience growth and release in our bodies, and the trees with their leaves, and the sun with rising and setting, natural business flows inward and outward. Each idea-seed germinates, sprouts, grows, flowers, fruits, and returns to seed and compost for the next generation of ideas.

The opposite of linear is not chaos.

The opposite of linear is cyclical.

So stop seeing productivity through a linear lens. See things in terms of rhythm and cycles. So many parts of business go in these cycles ... from prospect to client to alumni or from idea to development to launch. Or consider our own seasons of attention going inward to reconnect then flowing outward to express and experience, then back inward again. Our families have seasonal cycles of school and vacation, and larger rhythms of preschool, in school, empty nesting, and retirement. This is how nature works, within ebb and flow. Honoring this sense gives us a more feminine essence to where we put our attention over time.

Chapter 5
Outperforming Productivity and Time Management

Look, what I really want you to know is that it's not that you "can't" do time management or get organized. It's that **the people who have been defining the field aren't like you and don't live in the way you do.**

Efficiency studies came about during the Industrial Revolution, when manufacturing lines needed hordes of easy-to-control workers doing the same, repetitive task for hours on end: consistency, predictability, speed. Robots do that now on automate production lines. **What we need humans for**, what the world needs, is to bring their fully authentic unique selves to what they're doing, to follow what emerges from the inside rather than rules and structures imposed from outside.

Listen to your own biorhythm rather than punch a time clock. Yes, you still need to "work" to bring your unique gift into the world of form. To produce. To serve. But **the way we show up to do our doing is now based in our way of being**.

Discovering your own patterns that support your deepest desires is a great part of the fun. Work, or business, is a realm where we get to **learn about ourselves in motion**—not just intellectually thinking about who we are or what we want, but actually stepping out and seeing what comes up, the **resistance and the resilience**.

So feel free to toss out what you've heard about time management or productivity in a big corporate setting. Those systems themselves became a big part of creating stress through busy work and "shoulds" that actually worked against the grain for people like you and me.

It's time to experiment and **discover your own best patterns**, make processes of the best, and work out of the rest.

Compare Productivity and Purposetivity

Let's make it even clearer what we mean when we talk about what Purposetivity is and isn't by comparing it with traditional productivity.

First, consider the subtle differences in the goal each aims at. The goal of productivity studies and systems is accelerating the implementation of a goal. The definition of success is when you reach the destination. In Purposetivity, success is found in the quality of your journey. The goal of the approach is your alignment of experiential qualities with your fulfillment.

Productivity studies emerged in the Industrial Revolution and continued through the "time management" systems of the Information Age. It promotes increased production (from the root to produce). Purposetivity is attuned to the Transformation Age, wherein achievement is just one component of fulfillment. Because of this, the very definition of success is quite different. For traditional productivity systems, success can only mean continuous growth, whether in market share, revenues, or profit margins. Purposetivity includes financial sustainability, yet focuses on a purposeful quality of experience. It is more about how you embody your purpose in this realm of time and space. Think of success as upliftment.

Whereas productivity lends its focus to goal addiction by putting on blinders to everything save the destination, Purposetivity encourages us to be more alive in the moment, noticing the cycles and rhythms, even the apparent chaos.

The hallmarks of productivity improvements designed to maximize profitable expansion are consistency, predictability, and being in control and include concepts like "whatever it takes" and "commitment" upon which people can be judged. Showing up as a productive professional means leaving your emotions, family, and spirit at the door. Put on your mask and maintain your reputation and image. Purposetivity links every activity back to how it serves your higher purpose and the quality of energy you bring to engagement. Show up authentically and transparently as your fullest self, human and divine. Attunement and right timing carry more value in creating the larger experience than doggedly slogging through "no matter what."

This shift from a quantitative, countable, measurable characterization to a qualitative experience allows us to optimize for meaning and effectiveness more than optimizing time and motion efficiency. Rather than seeing time as an external (objective) and linear constant, we shift our concept and relationship to experience time in waves, flows, and cycles. Productivity keeps us busy. Purposetivity allows us to be engaged.

Productivity still has its places in the world. It is suited for left-brain, linear thinkers, who prefer to compartmentalize their emotions and areas of life. It works for jobs with repetitive days. If you enjoy structure (need someone to tell you what to do and when to do it), stay in the old system; it's not wrong for you. Diversity is delicious! Purposetivity is more for our right-brain, heart-centered businesswomen who yearn for a more wholistic integration of their One Life.

Shiny Bright Objects (SBOs)

The marketplace is full of "best systems" sold as the *only* way to reach your goals. Becoming a collector of systems or dropping something you've started in order to take on the next best system is Shiny Bright Object Syndrome (SBOS). The solution is to **focus on what's right for YOU**.

Once you have your big picture, that box top to the perfect-fit-business puzzle you're building, you'll see exactly how your most comfortable tools work together. Many of the advanced techniques you've studied will come into play—but later ... after you optimize for cash flow aligned with your style.

When you prioritize what to be looking at now and how your pieces fit together, you can easily exclude all the shiny bright objects. You save tons of money and time right there, not to mention reclaiming a huge chunk of your attention.

Unfortunately, as the internet marketing arena gets louder, we can feel "battered by experts." Everyone claims to have THE System, THE Formula, THE Blueprint. And curious entrepreneurs who are lifelong learners get intrigued by a whole lot of them! We have to recognize, however, that when someone sells an info product, they're fundamentally saying, "Here's my system. Let me teach you to adapt." Even filling in their worksheets and templates can become a place to hide from our own brilliance.

Yes, we all have tons to learn. There are far more things I know nothing about than I ever imagined! At the same time, it's important to be conscious and intentional about our choices when it comes to **investing our time, money, and especially our attention in those areas most aligned with our soul's intention** and its expression as our unique personal style.

Chapter 6
Your Personal Style and Flair

Your free Purposetivity Persona assessment reflects your productivity and leadership strengths and opportunities. It's great to have on hand as you complete this section of the book!
http://PurposeDrivenProcess.com/purposetivity_persona

You Are a Process

As it enters the world of form, that soul intention customizes the perfect personality to experience and master its qualities of expression. The core of **Purposetivity is honoring your uniqueness**. Where production-line productivity worked to make everyone a consistent, predictable robot, Purposetivity is based around discovering the precise WAY for you to do your doing.

The soul-to-personality manifestation is sacred and intentional. Here we're talking about your true character and tendencies rather than any drama training that lives in ego-land. Inhabit your personality consciously.

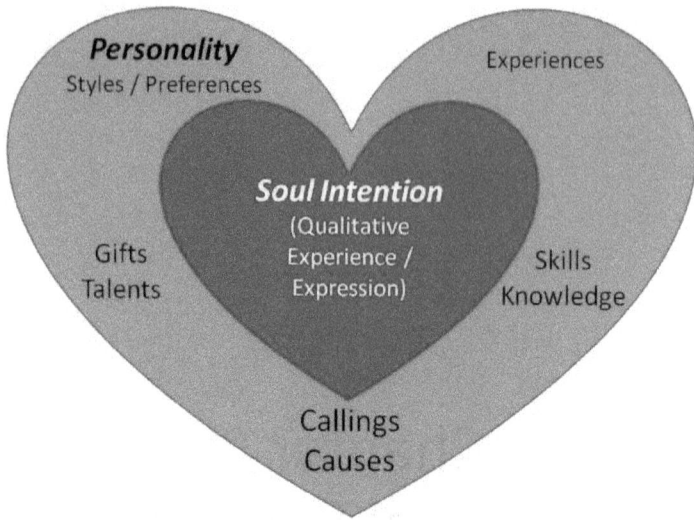

Our culture often assumes we have "a" personality, that there is an absolute "me," and it has to be understood (and redesigned). A root craving of humanity is to have something permanent, when in truth you are a process within the huge process called the Universe.

As women, we see through the fallacy in aspiring to consistency and continuity. We recognize the diverse inner roles, contradictions, and compromises. It's not that we "just have moods." **Women have an innate ability to tune in and turn on**—to tune in to the inner and outer circumstance, and to turn on the combination of elements that are most capable of interacting with the situation. Becoming more adept at higher choices is a lifelong journey.

Here's what I notice: sometimes I feel like doing one thing—maybe going for a motorcycle ride. Other times I feel like doing something very different—maybe getting out my watercolor paints or maybe diving into the computer and taking care of details. The thing is, every one of these is part of me. So what I notice is that who I am— my personality—is not one consistent thing.

When I try to take something that's very important to me in one moment and force that priority onto another moment, it's a form of violation. It doesn't let me experience the new moment and what it offers and asks of me.

32

So what I want is a form of self-management—**attention management—that allows me to feel into the moment in the context** of all the things that I love and matter to me, so that I'm still being true to my overarching values and goals while being aligned in the moment with the quality of energy that's available.

I can hear it now: "But what if I never 'feel' like working?" Ego tosses these thoughts into your space to distract you with exaggerations in order to create imagined drama. It's not real. If you have your own business and *never* feel called to do it, you're in the wrong bloomin' business anyway.

Shine on You Crazy Diamond

In actuality, we are a diamond comprised of many facets, and we need all our facets to shine.

Personality is not a consistent thing. Don't try to put yourself in a box. You are **a process of mediating between multiple internal desires and styles, facets of one diamond**. You have a lot of inner directions, and you are the *process* of integrating all of those and evolving to the next best expression of who you truly are. The important thing is to be able to express in a way that benefits the world, uplifts people, and makes a difference in the way things are done so that the whole world's next best expression can come through.

Among these facets, your **experience of reality is subjective to the personality of the moment.**

That's why your experience of life keeps changing. Different facets of your personality arise and subside. You are not a fixed constant.

So as we're taking a deep dive into your style and preferences, you can expect to find some overlaps and some contradictions. It's all welcome here!

Know Thyself

You can only match strategy, processes, and tools to your personal style if you know what it is!

In some cases, you may already have in-depth self-knowledge through a personal-growth system assessment you've done, such as Myers-Briggs or Enneagram. In other cases, your assessment can be more casual so long as it's conscious.

Trying to conform to a style/identity that was popular, recommended, or even effective in a different setting is counterproductive now. When I was a manager in a large corporation, we did a very large-scale analysis and training on the Myers-Briggs system. My employees and people in other departments consistently rated me highly in the attributes valued in the organization—logic, analysis, driving to results. Even my own assessment agreed!

But the truth was, these reflected only one aspect of all that I am, and continual conformance was exhausting and unfulfilling. **No amount of money could make up for being very good at not-me**. Burnout! Hence my exit from corporate employment.

Only a few years later, I took the assessment for a personal-development class. Guess what? My scores were not skewed at all. In fact, several were equally balanced among choices (part of my genius).

What was popular in high school doesn't work in corporate. What was recommended by academics doesn't work in practice. What was effective in corporate doesn't work in entrepreneurship. What's recommended in entrepreneurial books doesn't work in a blended lifestyle.

What IS going to work is to match what you do and how you do it to your own style at this point in your evolution.

YOU are the common thread!

Only by aligning your strategies, processes, and tools with your true nature will you be able to stick with it. You can feel good using your customized systems. They're no longer just a means to an end or a hated (or endured) part of your day. **The WAY you engage your work reflects exactly the experience you want** to be having and creates that quality of energy in its own right.

What's Your Style?

There are so many ways to slice and dice how you approach the world. You can learn something from each way of looking at yourself—something to keep in mind when choosing a business model, process design, or automation tools! The following models overlap one another and look at different kinds of criteria. Collect a kaleidoscope view of yourself.

Contrary to the Industrial Revolution view of the worker as a robotic, "always on" unit, real humans have biorhythms and moods and whole-life influences. Even our personality is not just one unit, but a collection of interests and (sometimes competing) preferences. Consider yourself an ecosystem: all the elements work in life cycles and provide checks and balances with one another. Or consider yourself a symphony with multiple instrument sections playing or resting to create the whole. Your signature is a unique combination, not quite like anyone else's!

Left brain/right brain

The popular model of the "right brain" processing artistic, spatial, creativity, and movement, while the "left brain" focuses on language, logic, and sequential tasks reflects very little about actual brain area function. But it is hugely useful when looking at our preferences for approaches and areas. There are no left-brain people or right-brain people, yet we have a sense of what we like and are good at.

Where do you consider yourself in the popular model of relying more on right-brain or left-brain associated functions?

Left Brain	Right Brain
• Speech, verbal	• Spatial, analog
• Logic, math	• Musical, artistic, poetry
• Linear, sequential	• Holistic, big picture
• Time, planning, control	• Patterns
• Detailed, accurate	• Creative, imagination
• Parts, categorize	• Symbolic
• Intellectual, rational, factual	• Pictures, visual, colors
• Literal	• Emotional, feelings
• Analytical, critical, decisive	• Intuitive, spiritual, timeless
• Practical, observable	• Facial recognition, non-verbal
• Cautious	• Adventurous

For free online assessments, consider:

http://testyourself.psychtests.com/testid/3178

http://braintest.sommer-sommer.com/en/

Introvert/extrovert

Another popular consideration is whether you fundamentally recharge your batteries by having time to yourself (introvert) or regain your energy by being with people (extrovert). This isn't a measure of shyness or confidence, or how much you love the people you love. We all love our people deeply! Introverts simply prefer smaller numbers of people for smaller periods of time. They tend to prefer conversation and connections "an inch wide and a mile deep." Extroverts maintain large numbers of connections, tracking what's current with more people. They want to talk it out to process what they think.

Where do you consider yourself on the introvert/extrovert spectrum?

Extrovert	Introvert
• Energized by being with people	• Energized by being alone
• Initiate and engage in conversation	• Listen more than talk
• Talk with anyone about anything	• Dislike small talk, prefer depth
• Talk to know what they think, bounce ideas	• Think before speaking, consult internal knowledge base
• Get bored easily, seek adventure	• Prefer writing to speaking
• Enjoy large gatherings and parties	• Dislike sudden changes
• Prefer people and things over thoughts and ideas	• Adore small group of close friends
• Knows a little about a lot of subjects	• Prefer thoughts and ideas over people and things
• Seek others during extreme stress	• Knows a lot about a few subjects
	• Withdraw during extreme stress

For free online assessment, consider:

http://psychologytoday.tests.psychtests.com/take_test. php?idRegTest=1311

Learning style

Each of us learns in a unique combination of ways. Do you like books on tape and remember everything you hear? Or do you need to see text or pictures to retain information? Or maybe things only make sense and "stick" for you when you've done it yourself, maybe more than once. I know my primary way to learn is to do, or at least take notes, thus running the information through my body. I am so bad with verbal information; I've even told my kids to send me an e-mail or text if they want me to remember some appointment or errand. Podcasts can't hold my attention because they're competing with the dialogue in my head (which is quite lively at times), so usually I shut the podcast off. But that's just me. What about you?

Number your preferred way to receive information from 1 (first choice) to 4 (last choice):

____Visual	• Slide • Picture • Diagram
____Auditory	• Lecture • Book on tape • Affirmation
____Reading	• Book, article • Lists and bullets
____Kinesthetic	• Do it with your own hands • Movement while learning • Highlight and take notes

For free online assessment, consider:

http://vark-learn.com/the-vark-questionnaire/

Social behavior style

This assessment is less well known, yet it forms the basis of many sales-prospect typing systems.

According to Merrill-Reid, social **assertiveness** is the degree to which a person's behaviors are seen by others as forceful or directive. **Emotiveness** is the degree to which a person's behaviors are seen by others as emotionally controlled. Flexibility is the ability to get along with people whose styles differ from one's own.

Where do you consider yourself on the assertiveness or desire to control others spectrum?

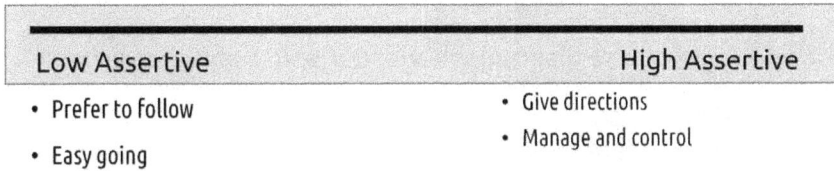

Low Assertive	High Assertive
• Prefer to follow • Easy going	• Give directions • Manage and control

Where do you consider yourself on the emotiveness or desire to control yourself spectrum?

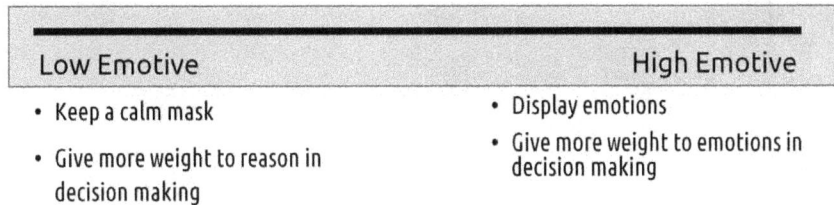

Low Emotive	High Emotive
• Keep a calm mask • Give more weight to reason in decision making	• Display emotions • Give more weight to emotions in decision making

Put together on a grid, they look like this:

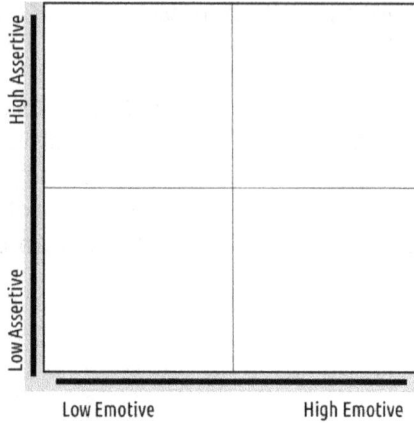

High Assertive

Low Assertive

Low Emotive   High Emotive

Place a smile on the diagram where your scales above overlap.

Here's a diagram showing how these quadrants commonly appear in their style preferences:

Driver   Expressive
High
• Results   • Creative
• Practical   • Energetic
• Solutions   • Friendly, Warm
• Fast, Decisive   • Vision
• Direct   • Enthusiastic
• Control   • Collaboration

Control of Others

• Formal   • Competent
• Logical   • Steady
• Avoid Risk   • Friendly
• Detail Oriented   • Mediator
• Organized, Plans   • Positive
Low
• Facts   • Team Player
Analytical   Amiable
Low   High

Control of Self or
Emotional Expression

For free online assessment, consider:

http://www.uwec.edu/CSD/grad/current/upload/
whatsMYstyleForSUPERVISORS.pdf

Multiple intelligences

Although Western academic systems generally focus only on intellectual skills, in truth, humanity possesses many more kinds of intelligence. You can be brilliant in areas that our education system can't value.

Rate your adeptness with the following as High, Medium, or Low:

☐	**Verbal-Linguistic**	• Word Smart • Reading, writing, listening, and speaking
☐	**Logical-Mathematical**	• Logic Smart • Classifying, categorizing; thinking abstractly about patterns, relationships, and numbers
☐	**Visual-Spatial**	• Picture Smart • Drawing or visualizing things using the mind's eye, pictures, diagrams, and other visual aids
☐	**Bodily-Kinesthetic**	• Body Smart • Touch and movement; may work best standing up and moving rather than sitting still
☐	**Auditory-Musical**	• Sound Smart • Creating or noticing rhythm or melody, especially by singing or listening to music
☐	**Intrapersonal**	• Self Smart • Independent, organized, self-aware
☐	**Interpersonal**	• People Smart • Relating to others by sharing, comparing, and cooperating
☐	**Naturalistic**	• Nature Smart • Learning about living things and natural events

For free online assessments, consider:

http://www.edutopia.org/multiple-intelligences-assessment

Standardized assessments

Standardized assessments tend to be deeper and more rigorous than a quick self-assessment. If you've used one for a job or personal development, by all means, bring it into the picture!

Myers-Briggs:

http://www.mbtionline.com/ $49

http://www.16personalities.com/ free

Enneagram:

https://www.enneagraminstitute.com/rheti-sampler/

Integral quadrants

According to Ken Wilber's Integral approach, we each primarily orient from a subjective ("I" or "we") perspective or an objective ("it") perspective.

To what degree do you give attention to and base actions on your inner experience (thoughts, feelings, memories, perceptions) compared with observable behaviors, states, tangible things?

Subjective/Interior	Objective/Exterior
• Prefer to follow • Easy going	• Give directions • Manage and control

In addition, we can each be more concerned with our singular world (what I feel, what I've done) or more with an aggregation (how we work together, how system elements fit the big picture).

To what degree do you give attention to and base actions on cultural expectations, relationships, and shared meaning compared with things singular to one individual?

Collective	Individual
• Keep a calm mask	• Display emotions
• Give more weight to reason in decision making	• Give more weight to emotions in decision making

Put together on a grid, they look like this:

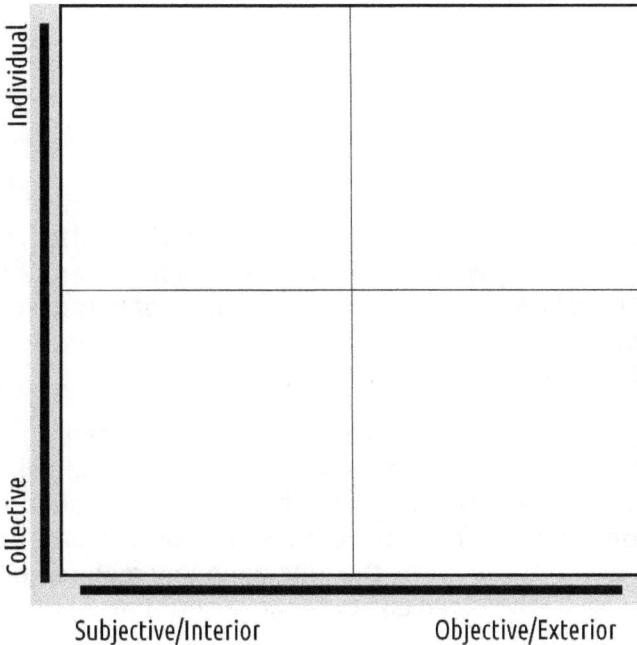

Place a smile on the diagram where your scales above overlap.

This diagram shows common characteristics and focus of attention shared by people in the various quadrants:

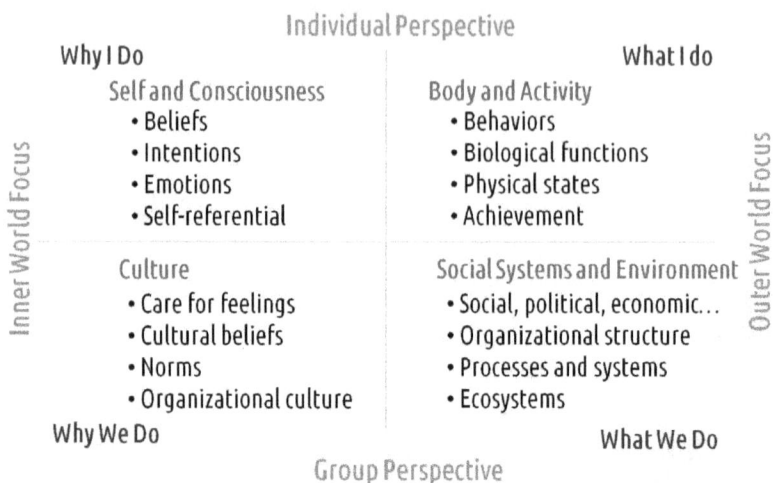

Individual Perspective

Why I Do	What I do
Self and Consciousness	**Body and Activity**
• Beliefs	• Behaviors
• Intentions	• Biological functions
• Emotions	• Physical states
• Self-referential	• Achievement
Culture	**Social Systems and Environment**
• Care for feelings	• Social, political, economic…
• Cultural beliefs	• Organizational structure
• Norms	• Processes and systems
• Organizational culture	• Ecosystems
Why We Do	What We Do

Inner World Focus — Outer World Focus

Group Perspective

Enjoy the Ebb and Flow

During each day, your mind-body's biorhythms rise and fall in various capacities. Learning what your best times are for different types of activities (and honoring that!) is a key element of Purposetivity. We are not machines, and we don't want to be. We want to **be fully human, in all our perfect imperfection**.

So start to notice your daily circadian rhythm. When do you feel most creative? Do you tend to be more focused and coherent in the morning, early afternoon, late afternoon? What periods of the day do you generally feel most like connecting with other people? Organizing your to-do list by the type of energy required helps you select the best matching activity to move your purpose forward at any given time.

Early Morning	• I generally feel
Mid-Morning	• I generally feel
Late Morning	• I generally feel
Mid-Day	• I generally feel
Early Afternoon	• I generally feel
Mid-Afternoon	• I generally feel
Late Afternoon	• I generally feel
Evening	• I generally feel

When do you generally feel most like doing different kinds of tasks?

Creating	Organizing	Detail Work
Follow-Up	Meetings	Client Sessions
Browsing	Learning	

For most women, our monthly cycle of shifting hormones also shifts brain chemistry. For me, it was pretty extreme. My PMS wasn't the attacking kind. My PMS left me feeling helpless and overwhelmed. Then during ovulation, I was manic. Until I recognized the correlation with my cycle, the back-and-forth drove my boss nuts. During ovulation, I'd be begging for more projects because I had excess capacity. Then I'd turn around and either raise red flags of risk to schedules or ask that other teams take on more work. Let's just say that wasn't effective for the team or for my reputation! Once I recognized the pattern, I learned to "wait out" the hormone cycles and to communicate only what would last.

Most women experience a time of outward expression and increased creativity during ovulation (often around the full moon). Then when the moon and the hormones wane, her state becomes more inward and contemplative. Neither is "wrong" or needs to be fixed any more than surfers would "fix" the tides to have no ebb and flow.

What you can do is be honest with yourself so that you can plan your business activities straightforwardly. No, you can't always honor the internal rhythms because other people schedule events. But you can attend to your rhythm as you go and choose your communication style and often your engagement level.

What about annual cycles of seasons and holidays? When you're creating a lifestyle business, there's no point pretending things are the same when the kids are in school as when they're home for the summer, or that the midwinter holidays from Thanksgiving to New Year's leave you just as much opportunity to focus on your business as ... March, for example.

What about That Feminine?

I know that coming from a male-dominated, high-tech field, I've been resistant to embracing my own feminine. And because my fundamental personality is more task-oriented and concept-optimized, that has seemed perfectly normal.

But in my aversion to "girly," I lost access to "womanly." I am simply not the type to wear ruffles and lace, to simper, or even to nurture much for that matter. Yet I am extremely creative, love my children dearly, can hold a friend through tears and laughter, and can be quite stubborn about inclusion and being responsively attuned. I just needed a language reset.

Here's what I did, and I suggest that you do it as well. I got out a piece of paper and made two columns, which soon became four columns. I started out wanting to compare masculine and feminine attributes, but I kept finding myself somehow resistant to and annoyed by what I *think* other people think of the feminine. (Yeah, read that again. I was resisting my image of what other people think. That's called "projection.") So what DID I think that they think? I added a column next to "Feminine" for "Girly," to note all of those "over-the-top" things that annoy the heck out of me—not that annoy other people, I was focusing on me. (We all have to own these things!) And if there's one on the Feminine side, there must be one on the Masculine side for "over the top." I drew that and labeled it "Macho."

Here's the start of my table. Please feel free to add more thoughts of your own!

Girly	Feminine	Masculine	Macho
Helpless	Empower self & others	Empower self & others	Dominate
Frivolous	Engaged	Hyper-focused	Bulldozer
Entitled	Responsive to shared reality, accepting	Premeditated	Demanding
Dependent	Attuned	Goal-oriented	Positional authority
Fragile	Vulnerable/strong	Strong/vulnerable	Rigid

When you have a good conscious sense of how you intuitively perceive the types, start noting where your beliefs and behaviors fall and which of those feel and work out best for you.

You're Still Evolving

Not only do all of these pieces of information *not* "add up" to any simplified pattern or archetype, they don't stay static. You are dynamic—growing and evolving—in response to an ever-changing environment of relationships and opportunities.

Don't worry about pinning each one down with finality. Leave space open. You don't live in conclusion-land. The objective is simply to bring more awareness to your own self and style in the mix of developing your business model. With this awareness of your nature in the background, designing your offerings and strategies becomes much clearer.

Chapter 7
What's Your Why?

While a Purposetivity *business* does express your soul's qualities on Earth, that's hardly the only thing we're here to enjoy! A fulfilling lifestyle also includes personal relationships, self-development, creativity and exploration, and deepening our connection with spirit itself.

Keeping in mind all that you've amassed about yourself, what other areas and experiences (qualitative as well as quantitative) would contribute to a wholistic lifestyle that is truly fulfilling for YOU?

Success on Your Own Terms

Before you can design your journey, you need to know where you want to head—you—not what the books say, not what some expert says. What is YOUR definition of success and fulfillment?

To have a business that supports a wholistic lifestyle, begin by looking at the qualities and experiences you want in each area of your life and the feelings you're creating with having them. Start with one area of your life, such as personal growth or parenting, and imagine it as a dashboard gauge for how it's moving.

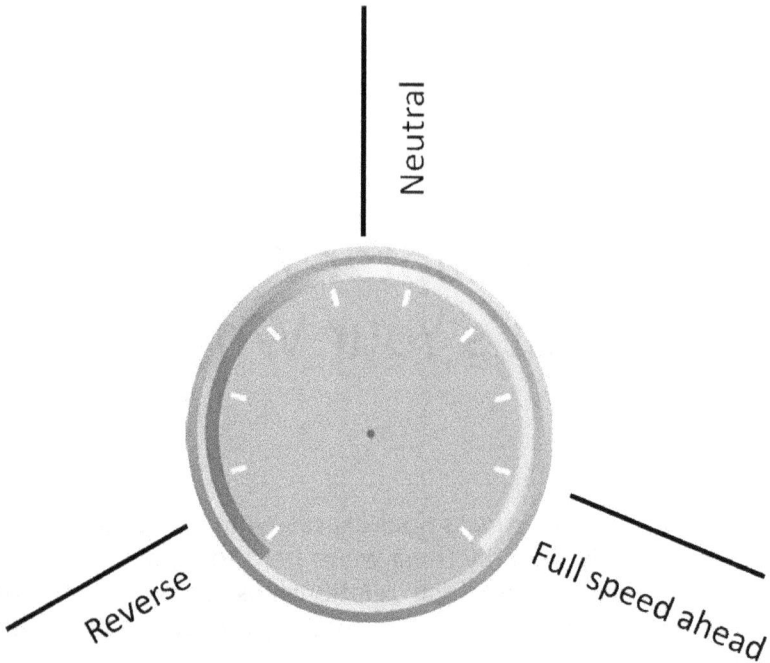

Neutral

Reverse

Full speed ahead

Start by sketching in a word or phrase for what it would look like if you had that area just the way you want it, "full speed ahead." Then add a word or phrase for how it would look if you were at a "neutral" point with it. Finally, identify what would constitute "reverse" so that you have your own red flag built in.

Here's one I did for my "Wellness Meter." Of course, yours will be unique to you!

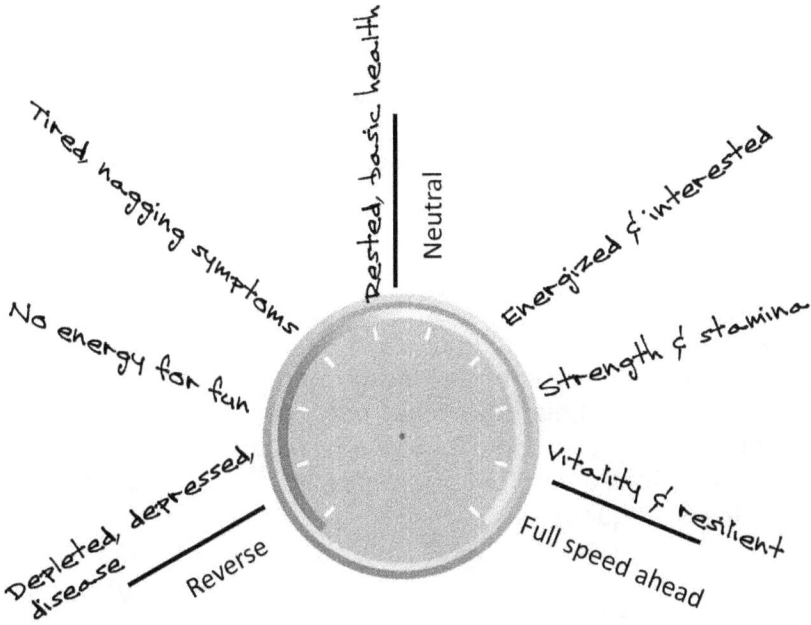

Now from your gut, put a line on your meter indicating your current level of fulfillment in this area. Just go with whatever feels right, a composite of different facets of what the area means in your life.

Make a second mark on the meter for where you'd like to be in a year. It may not be the ultimate for your lifetime, just what would be good a year out.

Write down two to three bright ideas for what you'd like your life to be like in that area in a year. (For example, "Energize myself by exercising for one hour, four times per week," or "Explore a new area of interest every month for a year by reading a book, attending a class, or visiting a different place.") Include specific activities and durations or frequencies.

YOGA 1HR/WEEK

MINI-TRAMP 3 MORNINGS, 10 MIN

Write down what seems to be blocking your light from shining through in this area. It might be time pressures, expectations, beliefs and thoughts, or physical constraints. Just make a note of what comes to mind.

YOGA 1HR/WEEK
MINI-TRAMP 3 MORNINGS, 10 MIN

EVERYBODY BUSY IN MORNING

Now take a deep breath and pause. Write down one or two key shifts you can make that would enable you to manifest in this area. You can ask for help, call in resources, or rearrange your approach. Open your inner horizon and see what appears.

YOGA 1HR/WEEK
MINI-TRAMP 3 MORNINGS, 10 MIN

EVERYBODY BUSY IN MORNING

MAKE LUNCHES AFTER DINNER
ALLOW MYSELF TO START MY DAY
AFTER THE SCHOOL BUS LEAVES.

Go ahead and do this for each area of your life.

You'll find blank worksheets of diagrams in your packet of gifts from http://www.PurposeDrivenProcess.com/bptemplates.

Here's the key: Review your desires and shifts across all areas to find ones that recur or conflict. Does it all hang together to create the balance that you want in your life just now? (This balance changes over time.) Is it reasonably feasible when taken as a whole?

And remember, you can't do everything first! Some activities actually pave the way to make others easier. Gently chart out which things you can and want to set in motion for each quarter (season) of the coming year. Remind yourself throughout the year to **think about what you DO want**! Once you get your personal task manager in place in later chapters, be sure to add an action item to start each quarter by reviewing your bigger picture. It all comes together!

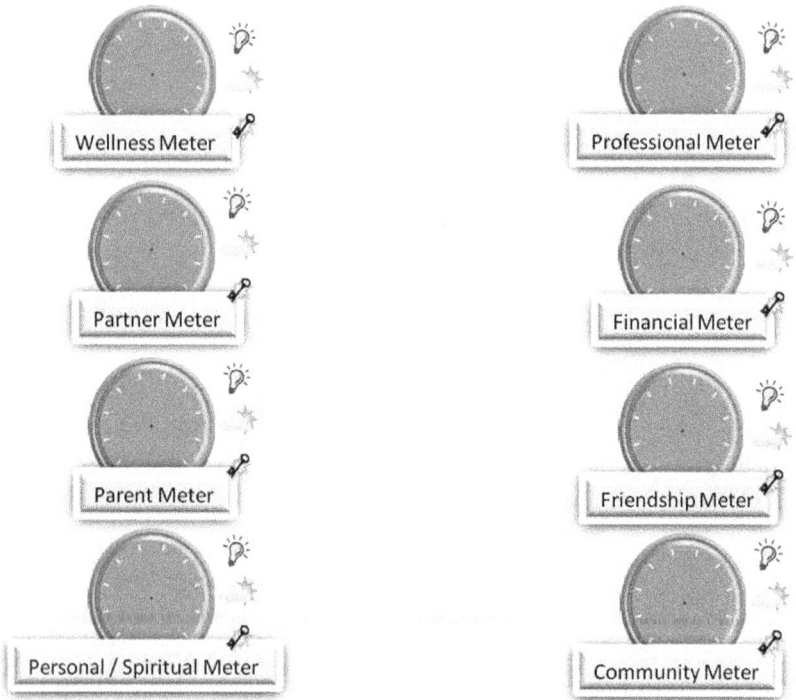

Wellness Meter

Partner Meter

Parent Meter

Personal / Spiritual Meter

Professional Meter

Financial Meter

Friendship Meter

Community Meter

Calling and Contribution

Too often people in the corporate world find themselves on a ladder to nowhere. They become so completely fixated on achievement and advancement that they are willing to sacrifice the moments of the only life they're living. The door to the corner office opens, only to discover after decades that the view is not all they had hoped it would be.

Your Own Business Is about Being Now-Here.

"What we seek is an experience of being alive, so that our life experiences on the purely physical plane have resonance within our innermost being and reality, so that we actually feel that rapture of being alive."

~ Joseph Campbell

The work you do and love is key to improving something on this planet. Part of expressing your soul's intention through your personality includes the **causes you naturally care about**. Developing the vision for the planetary impact and your mission for your contribution goes hand in hand.

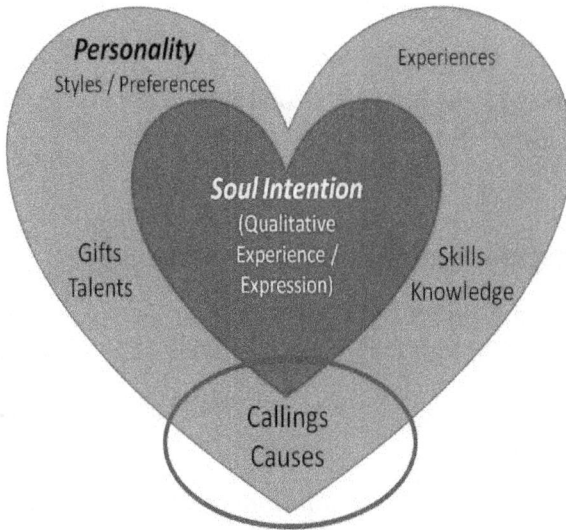

Life for Natural Causes: What Is Yours To Do?

Now it's time for you to articulate a sourced vision that expresses the essence of why you do what you do the way you do it.

Start by listing the causes you know you care about. Build the juice behind this by writing about conditions that make you angry.

What condition do you most want to see improved in the world for humanity, the environment, or innovation?

Now write about how your work contributes to improving that in any direct or indirect way. You may focus on one corner of the puzzle, but that's the segment of the work that is yours to do. When you do your magic with your clients, what is the result of your work? And how does that result contribute directly or indirectly to that cause that gets you going?

What would the world look like if that result happened everywhere, for everyone?

Building Your Inner Momentum

Deeper meaning vitalizes your daily business activities. Take your answers above and ask "What's important about that?" Then repeat with the answer you get. Repeat at least 5 times, like this:

"What matters to you in the world?"

"I want women to succeed in business while creating a fulfilling life."

"What's important about women succeeding?"

"Women bring a different perspective to the business world, a humanity that can make a difference."

"What's important about a different perspective in the business world?"

"We need innovative solutions that don't exploit people or the planet for the few."

"What's important about innovative solutions?"

"I want to create a world we can live in, rather than one that's dying."

"What's important about creating a sustainable world?"

"I want my kids and their kids to have the opportunity for positive life experience and joy."

Now you journal about the deeper importance and impact of the work you do, and how it spreads and expands to make a difference in the world.

Who Am I to Do This?

As you work with the "Inspired Vision" portion of your business plan (in just a few chapters), realize that this vision exists precisely because you are who you are! Part of your "story" is how you arrived at this mission. How did your life history perfectly position you to support it? Consider things you experienced that you never want another person to go through. Or consider the opposite: what gifts have you received that you feel every person should have?

A simple tool for you to consider what has transpired in your life history is Maslow's hierarchy. Here's a simplified version:

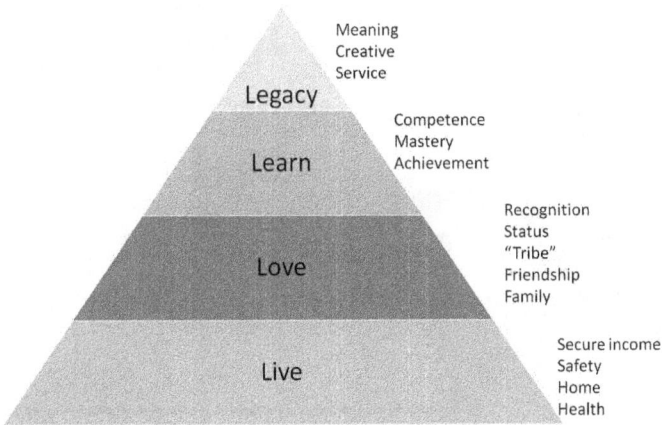

If you take those four levels, from bottom to top, and map out a timeline of your life events, you'll often discover the key elements of your story and what makes you THE perfect person for your mission.

You can put significant life events into these categories. A move as a child would be in the "Live" level, as would a major illness or surgery.

A death in the family would be on the "Love" level. Also, teen or adult dramas about peer groups and seeking approval are in the "Love" level. Certainly marriage and births also go here!

Graduating or taking ongoing education courses apply to the "Learn" level. Promotions or industry recognitions, advancement levels in martial arts, and any other "wins" generally fit into the "Learn" level.

For the "Legacy" level, include any time in your life when you had a major "aha" regarding your purpose, or a breakthrough in your sense of meaning. This area also includes any art or book you will leave to the world. Volunteering and working for social causes are other notable points in your life.

Take a few moments to gather significant events throughout your life and notice what level of the hierarchy they represent.

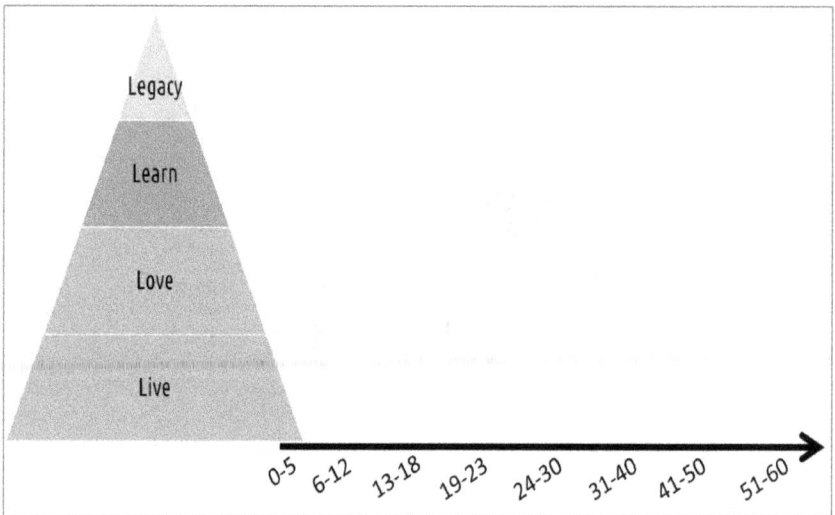

Just sketch in things like moves, changes in family dynamics, births and deaths, key relationship changes, and personal realizations.

Speak Your Passion

Now take what you've discovered and boil it down to the most powerful statement you can make about your vision and mission.

Here's an example using the vision I hold for the world:

> *I envision a world where every person experiences every facet of life as catalyst and crucible for evolutionary self-expression so that the Divine is fully realized and the transformations the world hungers for can come through.*
>
> *My role in this is to free the creative heart in business to focus on the things that matter to being on-purpose and have wider impact and better income, bringing more joy, passion, and aliveness to the world.*

VISION

I envision a world where _____ (who)

_____ (do what?) so that

_____ .

MISSION

My contribution toward this is _____

for _____ .

Create Your Purpose Prayer

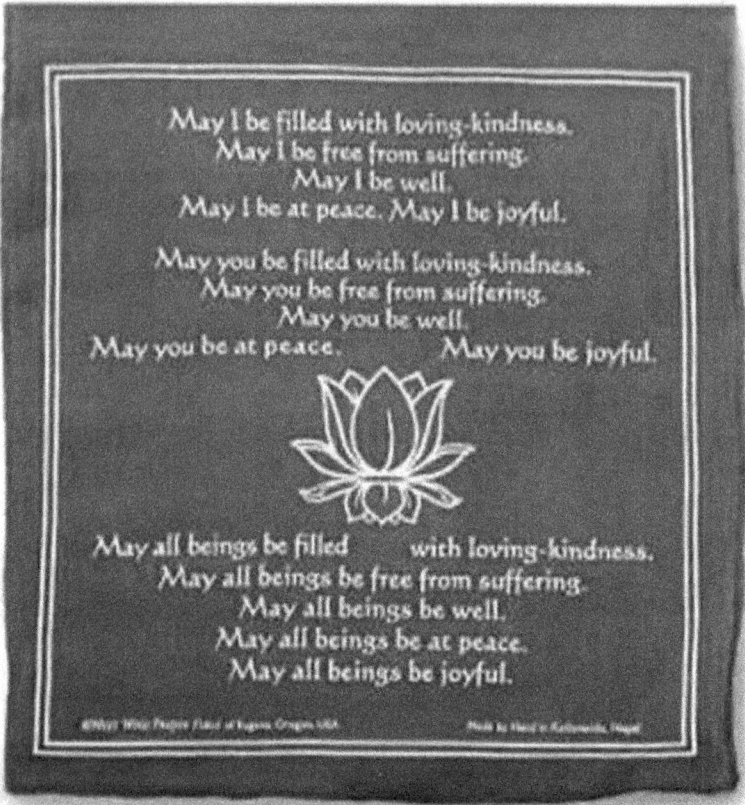

May I be filled with loving-kindness.
May I be free from suffering.
May I be well.
May I be at peace. May I be joyful.

May you be filled with loving-kindness.
May you be free from suffering.
May you be well.
May you be at peace. May you be joyful.

May all beings be filled with loving-kindness.
May all beings be free from suffering.
May all beings be well.
May all beings be at peace.
May all beings be joyful.

Use the format of the Buddhist Metta prayer to start your day with your mission. Suppose your mission were "to empower underprivileged children to express their creative instinct."

Start with intending your business transformation for yourself. We all teach best what we most need to learn!

May I be empowered to express my creative instinct.

Then intend precisely that for your target audience.

May underprivileged children be empowered to express their creative instinct.

And for the world:

> *May every man, woman, and child be empowered to express their creative instinct.*

Putting it all together:

> *May I be empowered to express my creative instinct.*

> *May underprivileged children be empowered to express their creative instinct.*

> *May every man, woman, and child be empowered to express their creative instinct.*

Now write your prayer here:

_____

_____

_____

_____

_____

_____

_____

_____

_____

_____

_____

_____

_____

Chapter 8
Your Radically Honest
Business Design

Before you buy into yet another "Six-Figure Success System" or "Seven-Figure Business in a Box," consider **what YOU really enjoy doing in your business** and the role you want to have in it. How do you WANT to be spending your business time? For that matter, how much of your Life time do you want to spend focused on business? It's time to get honest—with yourself first.

Too much of the entrepreneurial literature of the 1990s focused on a not-so subtle underlying message of "what I really want is to get AWAY from my business." Sometimes it was by delegating every-EVERY-thing to reduce the number of hours worked. Sometimes it was by removing yourself from mere craft and becoming expert at business mechanics. Often it was about creating a business *just* so that you could do an initial public offering of stock (IPO) with a seven-figure exit strategy.

What we want now is to *feel*—to do that thing we're passionate about—that makes us FEEL. We want to be IN our business, not looking for an exit strategy. Purposetivity is not about getting you out of the business so that you can do nothing. It's about you **doing the stuff that gives you the most joy and fulfillment IN the business** because that's what you choose to do, not because you have to do it (all). The experience of being in your business can be fulfilling and inspiring all the time.

This is where you bring those elements of who you are and your personal style into designing an overall business that feels great to run!

- If you're not a great lover of words and writing, you don't have to base your visibility on a written blog.

- Are you an extrovert who loves meeting new people? Be sure to include networking and learning events in your strategy.

The place where you collect all your information about the business you're building is called your business plan. For us, this is not just a plan for profit. Here, a **business plan is your plan for MORE LIFE— more joy, passion, and aliveness!**

Traditionally a business plan's intended audience was a potential investor. The structure had to be very formalized. You had to demonstrate long-term return on their investment, far beyond what is humanly predictable. Unless you really are requesting financing, that kind of business plan is just overhead.

This business plan is for YOU. (Even if you are requesting funding, this is a great place to start!)

Often micro-entrepreneurs don't think they need to document a business plan. If it's "just me," a business plan can feel like overkill. They don't know what to put in it. It looks like a lot of numbers and imaginary projections. But having **a place to corral your dreams and supporting information** does two primary things:

- It gives your left brain enough structure to calm down and stop questioning. You know you've thought it all through and there's a place to go back and find everything.

- It frees your energy to flow into creativity and heart connections.

If you can take some time to make a vision board and to identify your style, you can take part of your time to map your voyage. That doesn't mean you always think like a cartographer. It means the rest of the time **you can relax, trust the flow, and give your attention to your craft**.

Note: If you already have a business plan, use this section to reconsider how each area of your business matches your style!

Download template Evernote notebooks with the questions from this section so that you can create your plan as you go!
http://www.PurposeDrivenProcess.com/bptemplates

To have your business or professional expression included in your Purposetivity, your approach to the doing needs to match who you are. In Purposetivity, **both your mission and your strategy** (and your tactics when we get there) **align with your soul's intention**.

Always Documenting Plan B

Everything in the creative business plan presumes "this or better." You're not looking to definitively document an end-game and build dogma around that. **Business is a blank canvas, and the process and journey are your art**.

Today's business plan needn't be tomorrow's cage. Your business plan is a living document.

When I race my car on the track, I work my way up through the gears, fully utilizing the torque and power curve to gain momentum. First gear gives me the most "pull" to get things started, but staying in first gear would limit my top speed potential. When I have done all I can with first gear, I shift to second, then to third, and to fourth.

Setting up my line, or direction through and between turns, is how I guide that momentum. In a hairpin turn, I slow alllllll the way down, and I really have to crank the wheel around. But if I tried that in a high-speed sweeper turn, I'd spin out in a heartbeat. At speed, we use terms like "initiate" a turn and "squeeze" the brakes.

The subtle inputs in a high-performance environment are different from when you're standing still or getting started.

Your business plan, like Life, is **about movement, change, risk, and your evolution**. You evolve. The market moves. Times change. How do you set your business up to continuously listen, innovate, adapt, and respond in an ongoing spiral? That's part of why we'll set up the Quarterly Review in a later chapter.

Small business requires special leadership. It's up to you to **LEAD your own life!**

Recognize Your Stage in the Business Life Cycle

Each business has a life cycle from birth to ending, just as a human does. The current "age and stage" of your business determines which steps and tools are appropriate for now. Business experts all have their own ways of classifying businesses, but here's one that's a simple to use for starters.

Beginning: Stage 1

A **start-up** business is focused on getting the first few clients, determining the messaging, and figuring out how to deliver the result people are paying for. Usually it's a one-to-one delivery, or it's delivered educationally (teaching to a live group or through a webinar). The start-up business can get by with taking checks and PayPal, usually with a simple entry-level fee structure. Marketing at this point most often involves in-person contacts and business cards, perhaps with a website for backup credibility.

Rolling and Profitable: Stage 2

When you've got that rocking, you're in **stage 2**. You know how to get clients and are at least breaking even in your business. To do this, you may have created "segmented" offerings for different subgroups of your audience, and you may need to accept credit-card payments. You're working through your website (probably in addition to in-person), creating an e-mail list with an opt-in gift, as well as social media to encourage people to check it out. Happy clients and other businesses are referring clients to you. You have, or are looking to have, a part-time virtual assistant (VA) who can do some of the maintenance pieces for you.

Diversification: Stage 3

As this settles in, your business enters stage 3, "**Sustainable**." You have enough profit to support the business and your (at least minimum) lifestyle. You're offering a variety of products, potentially including recorded information products, group training, one-on-one coaching, and masterminds. At this level, many of your customers need you to offer a payment plan as well as a single-pay option. In addition to social media and probably public speaking, you're using blogging and even advertising to introduce people to you and your work. With your more advanced web technology, you can provide affiliate fees to joint venture (JV) partners. By now you have probably hired more than one assistant or implementer to handle the technical details. You need to ensure you and they have excellent communication tools and skills.

Empire: Stage 4

Should you want to build out from there, you can **expand** your business in stage 4. Some people call this the "Empire" stage. You have more clients than you can personally see, so you rely more on group programs and "evergreen" or recorded programs. You may even start to train others to handle some of the client work in-house. Your team almost certainly needs to include full-time employee positions and succession planning.

Legacy: Stage 5

When you are looking to create a business you can leave to your children, it can't depend on your presence. This kind of **legacy** organization needs to have a full staff of people who can do your magic, whether you hire them or license your program to them.

Here's a high-level overview of how I identify the stage of a business:

	1. Start-up	2. Profitable	3. Sustainable	4. Expansion	5. Legacy
Number of Paying Clients	1-3	Break even	Profit	Leveraging	Waitlist
Types of Offerings, Preferred Format	Individual or Teaching (Live or Web)		Both	Information Products, Evergreen	
Fee Structure, Forms of Payment	Single Fee Check or PayPal	Segmented Credit-card	Payment Plan		
Pipeline Status, Preferred Pathways	Hand Out Business Card, Network, Speak(?)	Web Opt-in, Social Media, Speaking	Blog, Advertising		
Partners		Referral	JV, Telesummit		Licensee
Team		VA (Temporary, Part time)	Implementer Experts (Consulting)	Employee, Permanent	Delivery Fulfillment Coaches, Departments

Chapter 9
Circles of Success
Business Planning

Whether you'll be wearing all the hats yourself or activating a team to manifest the mission, you still need to practice thinking from each place around the campfire. Each brings out a unique perspective, ensuring you have all the bases covered. Structuring your thought process supports you in seeing it through to success!

Most of us started our own business to get out of the corporate model of hierarchy and politics. The top-down structure and flow of rules just doesn't fit for right-brained, creative entrepreneurs.

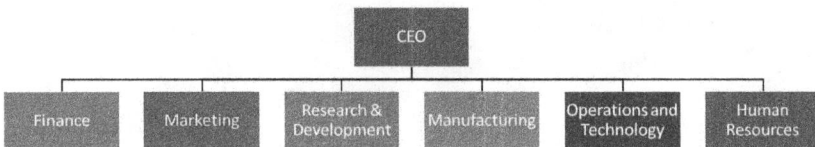

Purposetivity helps you shift from the traditional hierarchical organization chart, wherein "form follows dysfunction." You're also shifting from rigid boundaries and roles, dominance, and scarcity that create compartmentalized "silo" departments. In Purposetivity, everything is interconnected and directly proceeds from your vision and values.

Yet the same categories of considerations hold in any type of business. We still want to include those "departmental" perspectives in our planning. We don't want to miss some key aspect that can make our business flourish, so here's how we can take them into consideration in an integrative way.

Everything Revolves around Your Vision and Values

Rather than laying out the functions in a top-down hierarchy, let's take them and "wrap" them around the vision. In fact, make every area overlap with the vision so that you have one integrated business philosophy throughout all areas.

(Because this is a book, please just imagine these diagrams being animated!) First, the visualization starts to be more flexible.

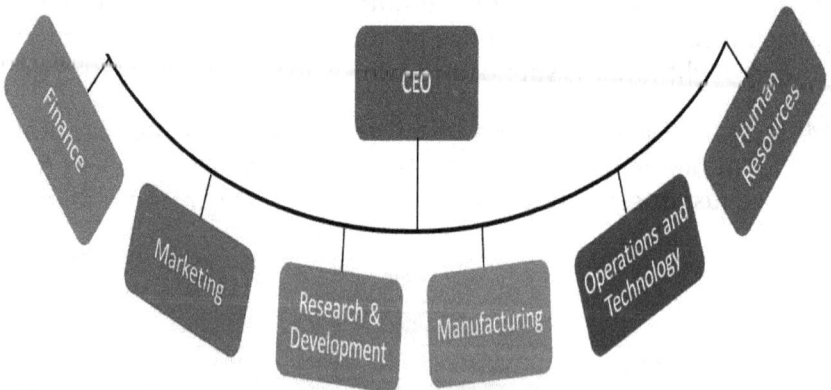

It flows to move the **vision to the center and everything else overlaps** and wraps around the vision. This provides an integrated, cohesive perspective on your business activities. Everything is related, and you can see it. If you have something that doesn't really fit, that's obvious, too.

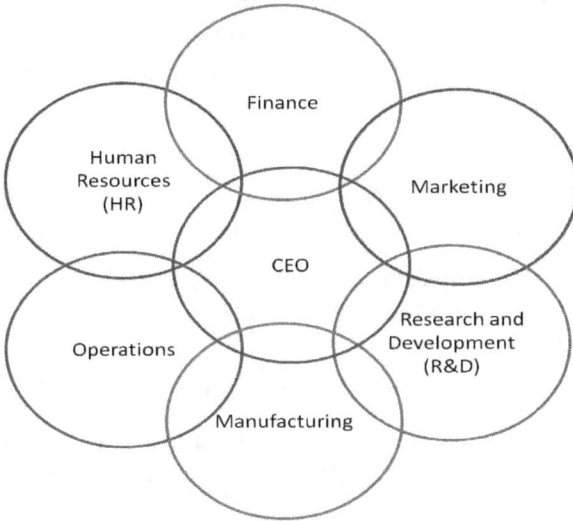

But those are rather mundane ways to label the functions as departments. What happens if we name them based on the purpose they serve in our business life?

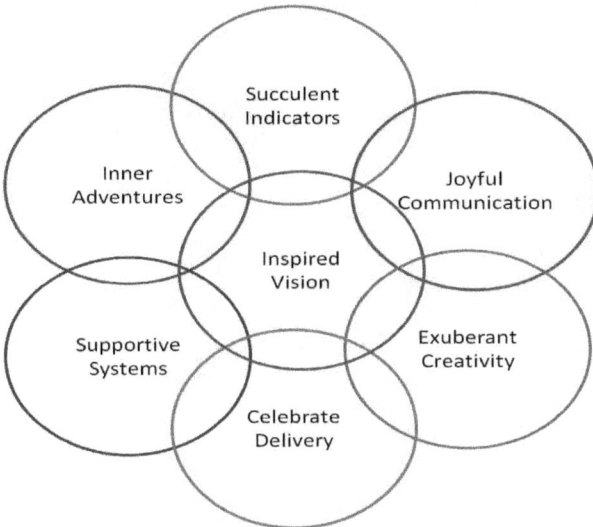

Here's a brief run-down to guide you through this section:

- **Inspired Vision** is the CEO role of your business.
- **Succulent Indicators** provide the feedback to keep your business sustainable, both in finance and fulfillment.
- **Joyful Communication** lets you get clear on who you want to serve and how you connect with them to build relationships.
- **Exuberant Creativity** is how you design and develop client experiences.
- **Celebrate Delivery** covers actually spending time with your clients or the purchase and delivery process for information products.
- **Supportive Systems** let you keep track of it all!
- **Inner Adventures** increase your depth and breadth of skills so that you evolve to bring more to your people.

Building a business plan, like so much around here, isn't a linear process. Please plan to cycle through it a couple times to get your initial structure set up and filled in!

Chapter 10
CEO as Vision Keeper

A CEO serves the key role of keeper of the (corporation's, stakeholders', and board's) vision and culture. While you don't need to hire a CEO, you do need to be able to think like one in terms of clarifying your vision, mission, and values in business.

Why do you do what you do in the world? Your Inspired Vision provides context for decision-making. **Vision provides context for BEing inspiration in action.**

Inspired Vision and Mission and Culture

You may feel called for multiple causes, yet this business addresses one. Here's where you make a conscious choice of direction, then articulate it clearly.

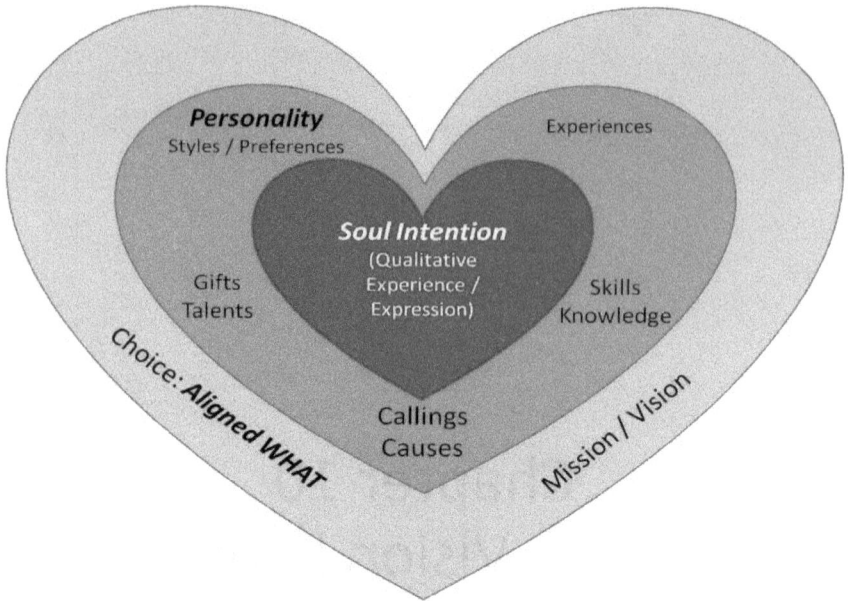

Your calling and contribution from your soul's intention lead directly into this.

As you articulate your mission and vision, consider these distinctions I learned from Ronda Renee:

Vision is how the world could be a better place and improve people's lives. Your vision is huge, far more than one person could accomplish. Consider it as a planetary team you belong to.

Mission is what your business does to contribute to that vision. Here is the piece that you claim and contribute to directly.

Here are mine as an example:

> I'm devoted to **transforming the fabric of society through conscious, awake leaders** innovating sustainable solutions that bring more joy, passion, and aliveness to the world.
>
> **MY role is to awaken and activate the feminine leadership** toward a consciously evolving economy.
>
> Place your vision and mission statements from the "What's Your Why" section of this book into the Inspired Vision portion of your business plan.

The Way You Do Anything Is the Way You Do Everything

With a clear statement of the problem you're addressing, the next step is to speak your truth in terms of how you want to show up in the business world. What are you exemplifying? What values drive your interactions?

Culture and values describe your *way* of doing business with integrity. Formulate value statements around **people, planet, product, process, and profit**.

When you address the area of People in People-Planet-Profit, include in your statement how you want members of your team to be treated and feel while working. How do you want customers to be treated? For that matter, include your other stakeholders like vendors and alliances.

In the area of Planet, what cultural values does your business demonstrate through your environmental footprint? You can consider everything from sourcing renewable energy to recycling.

Describe the primary source of profit in your picture. This is not just which clients or channels have the highest ROI, but on a deeper level state which resources you're accessing and how your value-added transforms the world. What qualities matter about your products and services?

Place your values and culture declaration into the Inspired Vision portion of your business plan.

Companies in the Conscious Capitalism movement provide excellent examples of purpose and values statements suitable for sharing to run a business.

- Whole Foods: http://www.wholefoodsmarket.com/values/corevalues.php
- New Belgium: http://www.newbelgium.com/brewery/company/history

Making Your Vision Tangible

Right-brain entrepreneurs often find numbers too abstract to really be meaningful or motivational. Here is a fun exercise, so get out your colors and scissors and make a status report you can hold in your hand!

Your download gift package contains a PDF of this pyramid to write and color on!

Setting up a visual, tangible self-feedback mechanism for these qualitative areas beyond profit could be challenging. But with a little creativity, it becomes a fun project!

First, we'll get a baseline. In the later "Quarterly Review" chapter, you'll see how to compare progress according to your subjective improvement.

Product Performance: WHAT

Draw a triangle with a scale up the left side to indicate in general "how well we do *what* we do."

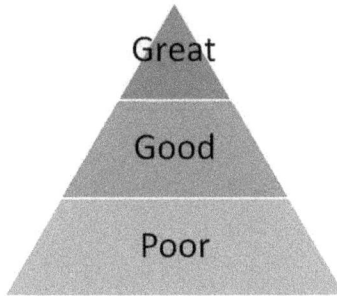

Great

Good

Poor

Draw a "waterline" for how full you feel you're doing in that area. No, it's not a scientific analysis. This is your own gut feel, first instinct.

Process/Culture Performance: HOW

Now do the same for a qualitative feel of "how well we model our *way* of doing it."

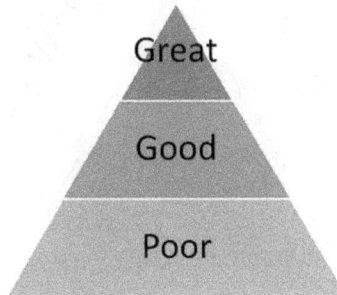

Great

Good

Poor

Draw a "waterline" showing how well you feel you're doing.

Vision Alignment: WHY

One more time for a qualitative feel of "how well we match our *why.*"

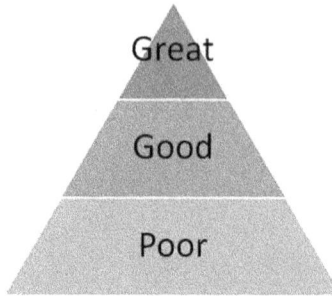

Draw a "waterline" showing how well you feel you're doing.

Here's the tricky part! These three are the foundation of everything you do in your business, so they need to fit together. It looks like this:

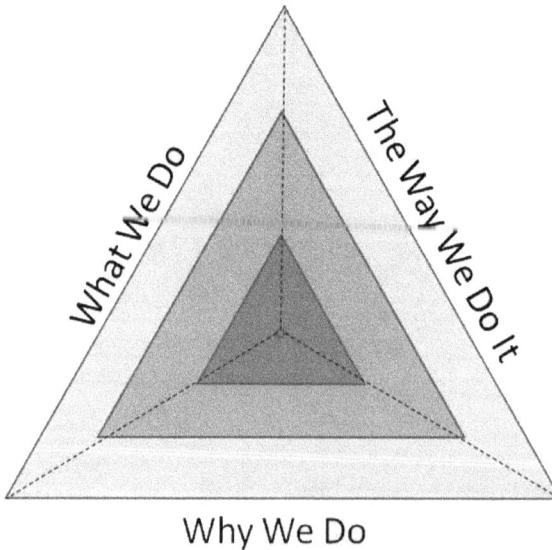

Transfer your markings toward the center point on each portion of the triangle-of-triangles.

Chapter 11
Make It Sustainable: Succulent Indicators for Feedback

Rather than a one-point Chief Financial Officer kind of CFO, this section of your business plan serves as your Chief Feedback Officer—financial and otherwise.

Don't get caught in the old-fashioned, linear game with only one way to keep score—profit. If you wanted just money, you could get a job. Why don't you? What are you looking for your business to provide in *addition* to profit? How else do you recognize that you're on track, making a difference, and having fun?

These are your **Succulent Indicators**.

Indicators ensure the business can continue its contribution to the world.

- Sufficient to support the business entity
- Sufficient to support your lifestyle
- Expansion to improve lifestyle, support others

What Do You Want to Build?

Remember this business exists in service to who you are and what you bring to the world. Don't get caught up in someone else's "idea" of what a successful business should look like. You get to set it up to match who you really are!

Some business owners set out to create an empire or a self-running business they can sell. Perhaps you are looking to create a legacy you can pass on to your heirs. You may want to become a recognized expert in your field, spreading your influence to new horizons. You could be building a community of like-minded change agents, or a source of jobs, income, and satisfaction for others.

Include the things you're looking for from your business beyond profit. Document how you'll know if your hours are flexible and you can run your business from any location. How will you know you've given yourself a meaningful creative outlet?

Once you can say how you'll know, you can recognize when things are not measuring up and when you're improving.

Beyond the Money: Multiple Bottom Lines

What do you want from your business that's not quantitative? Beyond the bottom line of profit (which is necessary to stay in business, but not sufficient to feel fulfilled) how do you know when you're doing well in other areas? You can consider: peace, passion, planet, playtime, and people.

Don't just give a generalized answer like "make a difference." Get underneath that. How would you know? What would it FEEL like?[1]

How do you want to FEEL when you're giving your service?

How do you want to FEEL when you talk about what you do?

This is one of the **key areas where the true feminine shines**. As homemakers and mothers as well as business owners, women already instinctively track multiple processes—meal planning,

---

1   Concept from *The Desire Map: A Guide to Creating Goals with Soul,* 2014, Danielle LaPorte.

laundry, kids' activities (when did they get quiet?!?), holidays, and gifting—then we get to business! Don't let society tell you you're "less than" if your kinds of intelligence are spread beyond math. You've got this!

Diagram Your Impact

Now set out your gut feel for how you stand on your bottom lines. You can use these diagrams if they match for you: Profit, People, Planet.

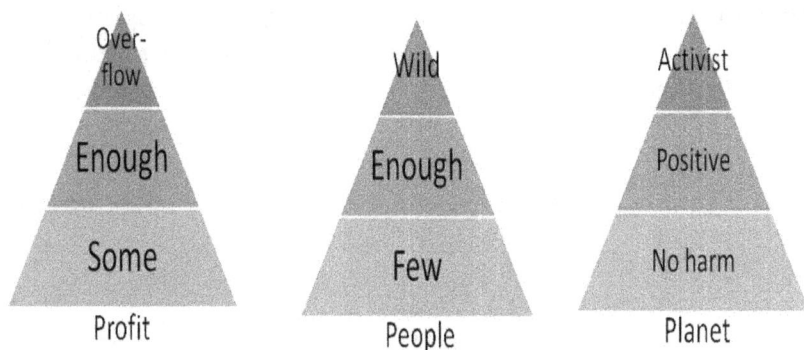

Profit — Over-flow / Enough / Some
People — Wild / Enough / Few
Planet — Activist / Positive / No harm

Knowing Your Knowing

You had some reason to put your lines where you did. Can you bring it to consciousness?

What are you considering when you look at each category? What would make it "better"?

What do you notice you have done or achieved?

How have you shown up?

What subtle contributions have you made?

Profit:

On a monthly basis, what is enough to sustain the business?

_____

> If you don't know, it's time to start tracking your expenses. Count everything from website hosting to lattes with prospects. You can use tax categories to set up an initial tracking spreadsheet.

What is enough to sustain your lifestyle? _____

Again, you'll want to track everything if you're not already. A simple program such as Quicken or Mint enables you to keep on top of things and definitely eases the tax-preparation burden! You'll thank yourself.

What is enough to allow expansion? _____

How much do you want to contribute to strategic philanthropy on a regular basis? _____

People:

On a monthly basis, how many lives do you touch one-to-one?

_____

How much impact do you create simply through your presence?

_____

How many team members are you supporting? _____

How do you contribute to alleviating social issues?_____

How do you connect people with each other?_____

Planet:

What percent of your waste goes to the landfill? _____

Are you and your travel carbon-neutral? _____

How do you contribute to improving environmental circumstances?

_____

Building Your Feedback Pyramid

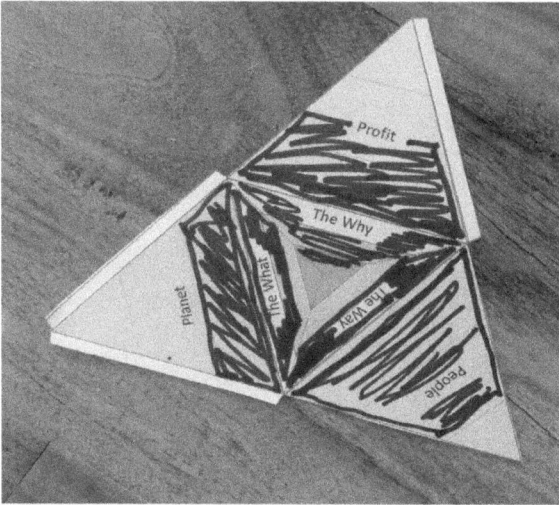

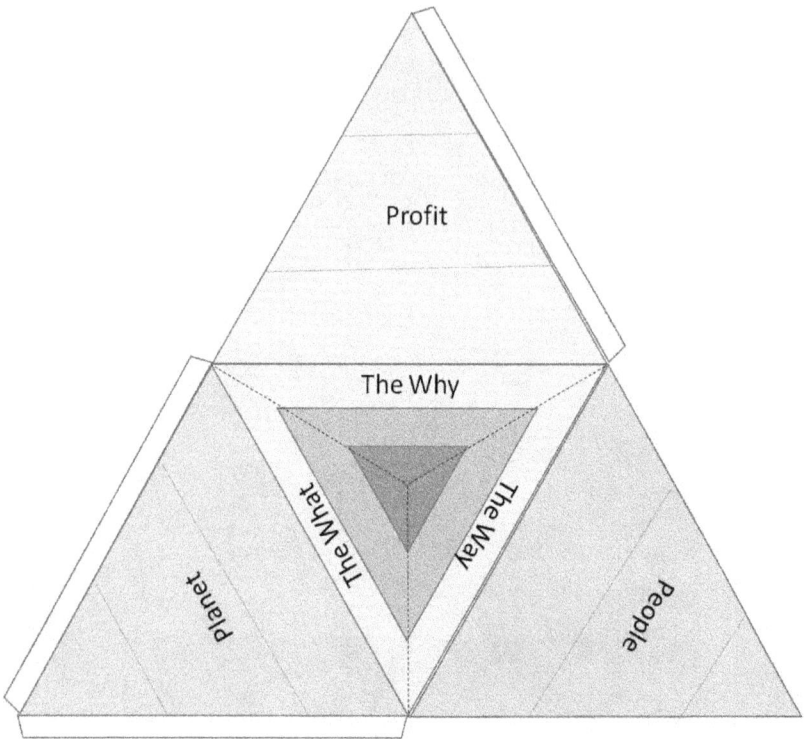

Building Indicators into Daily Actions

Choose the most important (to your sense of fulfillment and the continuation of the business) indicators in each category.

You can take each one of these indicators and break it down into a complete list of components. Then you "reverse engineer" precisely what you need to do to succeed for that metric. For example, to have ten new clients, you may need personal consultations with twenty people. And to have consults with twenty people, you may need fifty people in your speaking engagements. You'll learn over time what your actual percentages are.

For each one, mentally back up one step and notice what factors help raise the bar for that indicator. For example, serving ten new clients per week may be directly related to 100 social media exposures.

Finally, write down the inspired actions—things you can actually do—that connect directly to improving your sense of fulfillment in your business! Include their frequency (daily? Weekly?) to set the whole chain in motion for your business.

	Indicators	Influencing Factors	Inspired Actions
Profit	1. 2. 3.		
People	1. 2. 3.		
Planet	1. 2. 3.		

These types of "lead-in" numbers give you precise guidance each week as you set your intentions. They become the repeating actions in planning your to-do list. This way each of your activities actually leads into the results you're looking for and you avoid wasting time (and money) on random busyness.

Pro Bono Work

We all meet immensely talented people who could benefit from our work, but who don't have the funds to pay for it. Occasional bartering can be a boost for both parties, but long-term bartering can't pay your mortgage.

Yet we still feel called to give.

A clear way to handle this instinct to help is to create a "pro bono waitlist." Determine what percentage of your clients you can take on pro bono and still keep your business sustainable. It may be 5% or 10%. Let's use 10%. For every ten paying clients you enroll, invite one motivated person from the waitlist to work with you at no charge.

Removing Clutter

Some of the activities in our current business are there just because of habit or hearsay. Someone told us the "75 Things You Must Do to Succeed," or the activities are remnants of the way we started when our business was young.

Review your current to-do list and calendar and note any activities that you can't relate directly back to your own fulfillment and "conditions of enoughness" as Jen Louden calls them.

Make a plan to exit those activities gracefully.

Dashboard Review

You'll be coming back to look at how you're doing, both quantitatively and qualitatively, in your reviews that we'll design in a later chapter.

Chapter 12
Let People Know You Love Them: Joyful Communications

Remember your vision for the world as a better place? And your mission for impact in one corner of that? Look back now and identify the **key group of people you can serve** to move that mission forward, in the direction of your vision for a better world.

How do you match your style and preferences to reach out in **Joyful Communication**?

The goal of this section of your business plan is clarity in ensuring your delivery meets the outcomes your people desire.

It's not about "where's a big market that I can sell my stuff?" **Purposetivity is about "how can I bring my gifts to bear on the problem space I feel most connected with?"**

You don't have to have achieved the top mark of proficiency in the area you're coaching. You don't have to be all perfect, right, and done. Most Olympic coaches have not earned gold medals, but they have powers of observation and feedback to draw the best from their clients.

Your clients don't have to be people with whom you'd like to be best friends and hang out Saturday afternoons. They are people who most benefit from the assistance you provide AND whom you most enjoy being with and delivering out into the world. Consider these areas:

- Community you know well

- Problem you've solved yourself

- Demographics: What do you know about their age, income, gender, etc.?

- Psychographics: What do you know about their concerns, likes, tendencies, etc.?

- What is their pain? What problem do they have?

What do they really want, and how do they want it? (Hint: they don't want "a session." They have a *reason* they're coming, something they want improved or solved!)

What are you *really* offering them?

Ask Your Avatar: "Tell me about yourself"

While marketing used to be about creating a problem so that you could solve it, now you get to use this space to reach out and get to know your people. There are people specifically *looking* for the type of service or product you provide. They've reached "that point," and they're ready to get beyond it.

Imagine yourself talking to your ideal client. What do you notice? Really, take a few minutes and close your eyes and imagine yourself having a delightful drink (coffee, wine, whatever!) with the exact person you'd most love working with.

Ask them about their situation and take notes.

Ask them about their wins and dreams.

Ask them about their challenges and frustrations.

Ask what would most help them right now.

Ask how they'd like to find out about that. And how they'd like to receive it.

Now write down what you discovered directly and what you "gathered" about this client in general.

Sometimes they have consistent attributes about where they live, how much they make, their family status, age, and education.

_____

_____

_____

_____

Sometimes they are grouped together more by their personality type, preferences, and style; by their dreams and their progression in working toward them; or by their attitudes about the world and themselves.

_____

_____

_____

_____

If your audience falls into obvious subgroups, what differentiates them? How does it affect what they're looking for or how they want to receive it?

_____

_____

_____

_____

Of the groups and subgroups, which are you most excited to work with (three or fewer)?

_____

_____

_____

_____

Describe where they hang out.

_____

_____

_____

_____

How would each group describe The Thing they want improved? What do they rant about when talking with their BFF?

_____

_____

_____

_____

What impact or follow-on pain does that cause in other areas of their life?

_____

_____

_____

_____

Designing Joyful Communications: Begin with the Big Picture

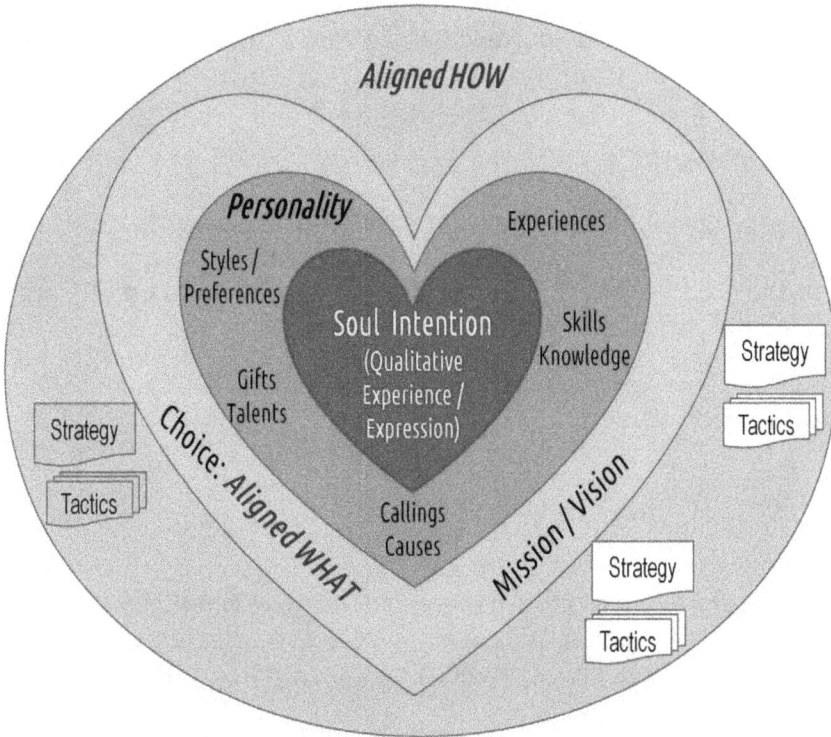

Not every type of activity fits every type of person! Here's where you get to design an overall business model and marketing strategy that feels good for you.

- Hate to write? Leave blogging O-U-T!

- Love speaking to groups? Put public speaking near the top of the list!

- Pick only the ones that look like they'll lift your spirits to implement—because **when you're happy, you're hot!**

So grab a big, blank piece of paper. Draw dotted, horizontal lines that roughly divide it in quarters. This is just your starting sketch, so don't bother with perfection. We'll think it through from the bottom to the top.

Do not draw in anything that feels like it's not you. I don't care how many silver-bullet peddlers have said *xyz* is the magic answer to build "every" business. **You, and your ideal people, only need to meet in spaces that make you both happy**.

The quality of your journey has to match the quality of your destination!

Deepest work

For your Big Picture, at the bottom of your paper, write down the way you most dearly want to serve your mission. If it's one-on-one, put that in a big heart. If your ultimate objective is to create large online deliveries, put that in a golden box.

You may have some of each at your "top end," so you can put them next to each other.

Which Is the best solution for them?

Just before someone signs up with you, chances are you have some kind of sales discussion with them to determine whether you're the best fit for each other. Whatever you call this, a "strategy session" or a "creative consult," or something else, put it in a box above the outcome they would sign up for.

Draw an arrow from the discussion to each possible enrollment. Draw one more arrow off to the side and label the end "Not a fit at this time."

Come talk to me

How do you encourage people to have that conversation? In the long run, you may have multiple avenues "in," but for now just note two or three ways that someone could be invited to a strategy session.

- The closing page of an e-book or paper book
- The final slide of a webinar preview
- A handout used when speaking to a group
- The closing comments of a recorded product

- Reading your web site

Draw the top two or three you want in place early as circles in the section above the strategy session box.

Draw arrows from EACH of those circles to the strategy session box.

If any of the items clearly references another (like you're speaking to a group and have a book for sale at the back of the room), draw an arrow showing the direction of your prospect's attention flow.

Hint: When you create these pieces, make sure the invitation to the strategy session is the **obvious next step** for someone to take toward meeting their desires.

Awareness building

So how does someone even find out about you? How would they know to get into one of those "find out more" pieces?

Networking meetings

- Professional organizations, forums
- Meet at an event, education
- Social media: Are they Facebook or LinkedIn focused? Are they Googling for services like yours (mass market) or looking to friends and trusted advisors for referrals?
- Newsletter
- Trades, guest blogs, articles
- Telesummit speaker, panelist
- Book or anthology
- Referrals

Do you enjoy writing, speaking, or networking? How do you FEEL when you do those things?

What really drains you—just the thought of it makes you want to go back to bed and pull the covers up over your head?

Which **best matches the experience you want to be having?**

Again, draw in the top two or three you want in place early. When you implement them, make sure it's always clear that someone's **obvious next step** is to go to your website or your next talk!

Draw the arrows in for what you would have people do next, most likely go visit your website to see what's up. Sometimes though, you'll be using these specifically to promote your next group delivery or webinar.

Here's a sample diagram, developed from bottom to top, but which customers experience from top to bottom:

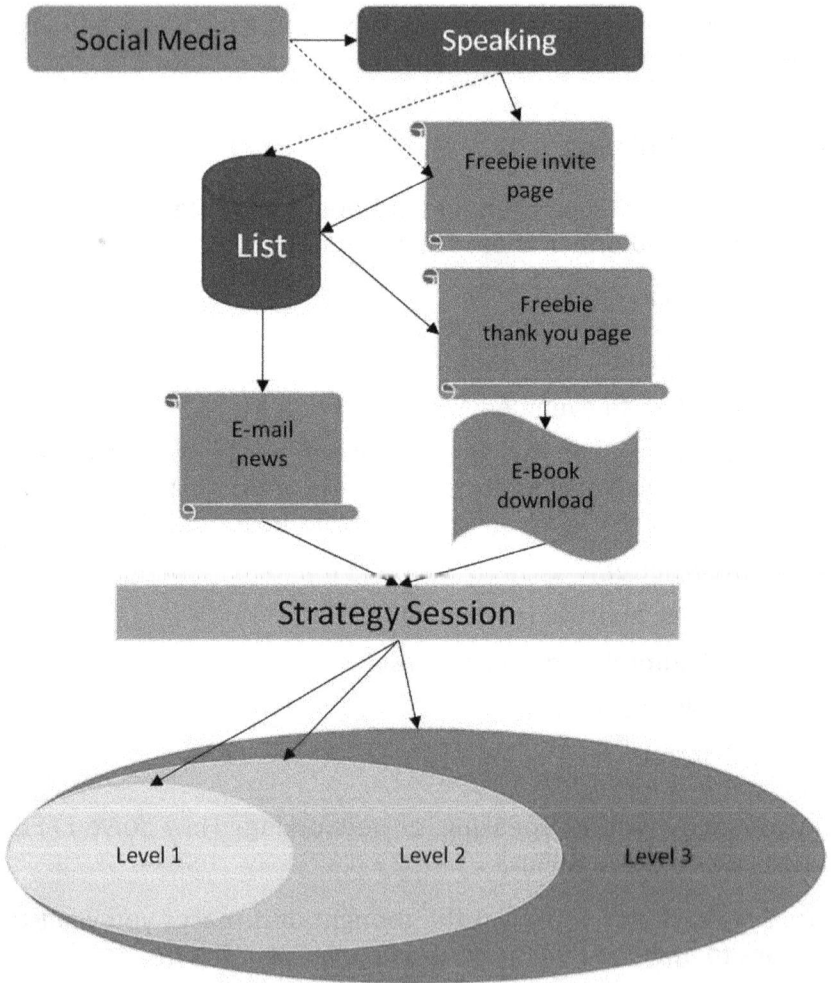

Homework: Market Research

Now ASK Them!

Contact at least ten people in your target area and ask if they'd give you one hour to *help* you grow your business. Invite a few key folks who represent your audience over for a potluck focus group or ask people if you can buy them coffee and interview them for your research. At the very least, create a quick survey on surveymonkey. com and request that people take a few minutes to give you important information. You can ask them questions like:

- What do you want?
- What are your challenges? What gets in the way?
- How does that impact other areas of your life?
- How do you feel inside when that happens?
- What would life be like without that?
- How important is it to you to resolve this?
- How much money would it be worth?
- How much time would you invest?
- Do you prefer one-to-one or group? Phone or live?

When you design an offering from this, how likely are they to be interested? Give them a VIP invitation to your launch!

I Can Help You with That!

Express the transformational outcome of working with you. The outcome is always the same, regardless of how you deliver it. Some may receive the transformation through one-on-one sessions while others may participate in an online group webinar.

Features: What you do / talk about / activities	Benefits: How their experience is better for that	Outcomes: How their big-picture life experience is impacted by having that benefit

What is the result/outcome of having worked with you?

What is the transformation in someone's life?

How does that touch other areas of their life?

- Finance
- Family
- Fitness
- Faith/Spirituality
- Focus

Refer back to your Inspired Vision and use your answers to the "Why is that important?" exercise.

To let someone know you can help, you generally answer the common question, "What do you do?" Keep in mind that this question really isn't asking about or focusing on features or modalities you use. What someone really wants to know is **what you can do to improve their experience of their life**.

Here's a good format to use if you don't already have a favorite:

> "You know how some [___insert target market descriptor ___] have problems with [__insert common symptom or pain___]? Well, I [help | teach | support] them to [___insert

ultimate outcome of transformation ___] without [___the thing they fear that holds them back___]."

Alternatively, you can use this form:

"[__ insert target market descriptor with problem___] hire me to [___insert ultimate outcome of transformation ___] without [___the thing they fear that holds them back___]."

MEMORIZE THIS, or a couple versions. Practice in front of a mirror.

Chapter 13
Designing Customer Experiences to Maximize Results: Exuberant Creativity

For all or those bubbles you drew in Joyful Communications, this section of your business plan is where you get to design and develop the content to go in them. What are the sessions you give? What content and exercises fill your workshop agenda? What topics do you blog about?

This is the playground for **Exuberant Creativity**.

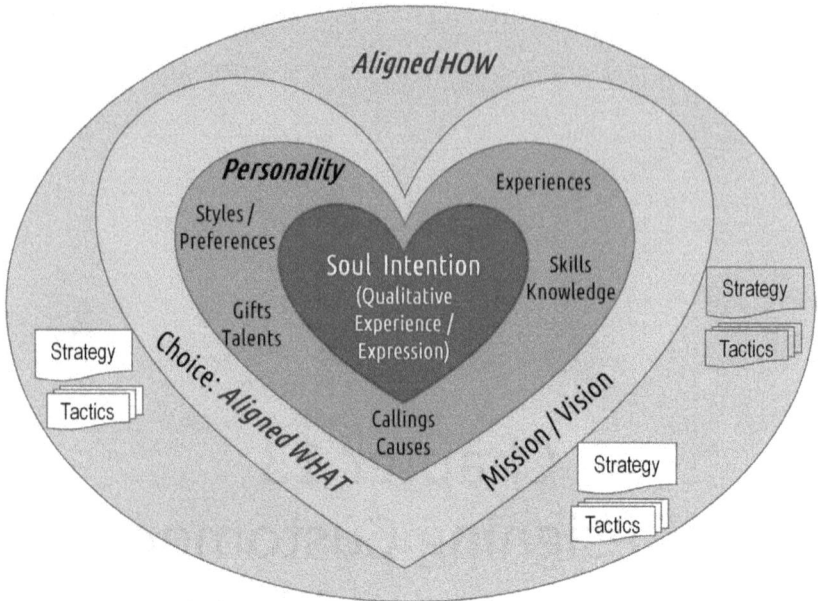

It's time to get very clear and specific about **how you most enjoy serving your clients**. What matches your personal style and intentions?

- Do you love the creative expression of writing? Design blogging or a book into your flow.

- Do you love playing with pictures and colors? Here's where you get to design layouts for flyers, slides, handouts ... even your website if that's your cup of tea!

- Do you love leading a room through a group experience? This is your R&D space to develop your curriculum and agenda, as well as the exercises folks will do.

Get very clear on which delivery mechanisms make you happy. Then verify with your vision—are you in alignment? If not, what needs to be smoothed out or re-examined?

Go back to your Big Picture and review what you have at the bottom as your "Deepest Work." Also note each piece of content (e-book, workshop, talk) that needs to be created to feed into that.

Begin with the End in Mind

Starting with your promise, the result of having worked with you, how would someone know they "got there"? What **quantitative and qualitative experiences** would they have? What would they be able to do (observable behavior) that they'd not done before?

Using whatever medium (written, spoken, video, interactive group, or one-to-one) lights you up, take one step backward and ask, "What would they need to be able to do or know for that result to happen?" You may have a list of three things or thirty (which would be multiple programs!).

Write down (perhaps on sticky notes) each way you could deliver your outcome, across all delivery methods. Then you can rearrange them to map how one can lead into another.

For each of those items, step it back again until you've designed a bridge all the way back from where they want to be to where they're actually starting.

Identify Package Milestones

Group the elements of your design into packages that each move a client from a known starting point to a recognizable milestone that has value in itself. Each one also sets the client up to be perfectly prepared to embark on the next stage of your journey in a follow-on package.

Sometimes you'll create "parallel" packages or bridges between the same start and end points! This enables you to take advantage of clients' learning preferences and adapt to their budgetary constraints. In general, a self-paced program allows people to get into your work at a lower price point, whereas you can charge more for more personal time with you. They are simply two delivery mechanisms for the same transformation.

Build It Forward

Now you can start with those initial pieces and create the actual materials (visuals, scripts, worksheets, whatever!) to support creating each step of the journey to the results.

Plan your design and development time into your calendar for your most creative slot in your daily biorhythm.

In the chapter where we set up your calendar and to-do manager, you'll circle back here to enter everything that needs to get done. (Remember, it's not linear.)

Prototype and Adapt

One reason to "build it forward" is that you can start selling the beginning pieces immediately.

Gather clients who are ready for that stage of the journey and offer a "seed launch" of the package or program. In exchange for a lower price point and giving feedback and testimonials, they get access to the results NOW.

Find out early what's working and what's off target so that you can adjust for maximum results for your clients on the full rollout.

Chapter 14
Delivering on the Promise:
Celebrating Delivery

Now that you've designed the way you want to work with people and developed your solution(s), it's time to engage! Actually providing your results in a way that creates more joy, passion, and aliveness for everyone involved is definitely cause for **Celebrating Delivery!**

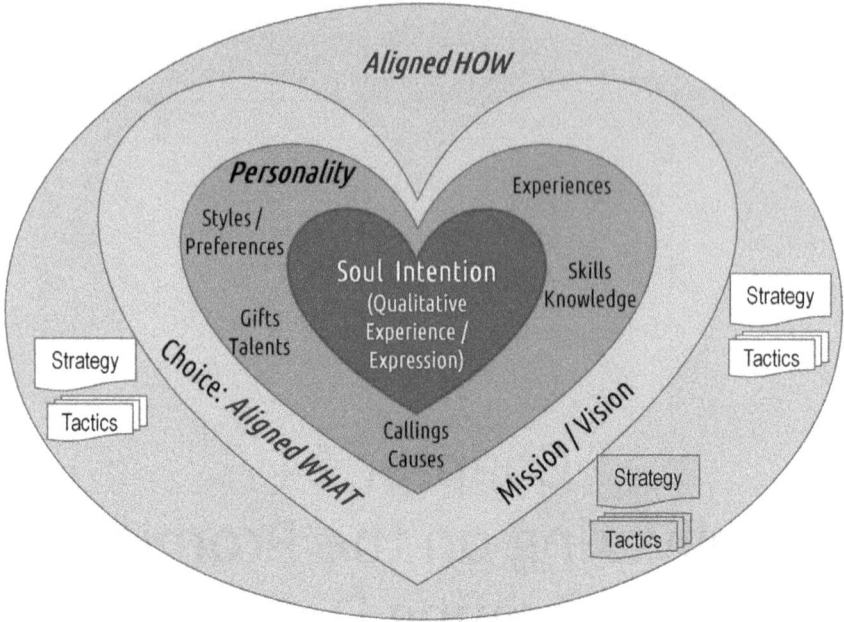

A traditional work-month has twenty days or 160 hours for employees. You can set your baseline for how your overall lifestyle works.

How many hours per month do you want to spend on your business?

How many of those hours will actually be delivering to clients (not marketing, development, copywriting, technical, or finance)?

Hint: Work this section showing what you want in the next three months, then again for what (you currently think) you want in one year. It's a growing game.

How Many Clients Is a Full Practice?

Reality check: How does the number of hours with clients compare with the number of work hours you want to be spending? Does it fit with your overall vision and your sustainability indicators (enough to support you and not so much that it burns you out)?

Add up the number of unique clients you'll be serving each month. Consider that if you package your sessions quarterly, you won't have brand-new clients in every slot every month. Sometimes marketing group programs widely makes sense, especially if they are online and have "infinite" capacity. But for one-on-one work, you won't need to reach thousands of new people per month. **Mass marketing is rarely necessary for customized work.** Review your marketing section to make sure it matches these goals (as well as your style).

Celebrating Milestones and Completions

What do various levels of celebration look like to you? Sometimes a good whoop at the computer screen is all you need. Or chocolate. **Never underestimate the celebratory benefit of chocolate.** You might celebrate with a call to a friend. Or invest in a book or training you've been wanting. For big milestones, go ahead and have a big celebration—launch completion dinner or weekend at that hot-spring resort!

Celebration Brainstorming Sheet

List several ideas you'd love at different levels of celebration.

Size of Accomplishment	Body	Mind	Heart / Soul
Small			
Medium			
Large			

Be sure to include celebrating in your "treasure map" of processes and timelines!

Celebrate Improvement

The celebrations you outlined carry real weight in activating your engagement with Purposetivity. Implement them! Making yourself empty promises and moving your own carrot are demoralizing. You need to be able to **trust you first**.

In addition to milestone celebrations for things well done, teach yourself to recognize and acknowledge when you take those steps that are difficult for you, when you expand your comfort zone by stretching your edges. Appreciate when your fluidity improves in your process or interaction. You can be the first to beam out, "Go ME!"

Model Generative Boundaries

When you do fantastic work, your clients love you. And you get more clients. And they want more of you. They want your perspective—on every little thing. Right. This. Moment. You can end up with an overload of follow-up work and clients calling you at all hours.

You want your customers happy. You want testimonials and referrals. You both truly care and feel you "should" do more. "Should" be available. Always on-call.

Not.

That's **Entrepreneurial Quicksand**. You'll go under.

It starts with work activities insidiously eating into your personal time. You stay up a little later and miss some sleep. Then a little more sleep. Then it's meals. Time to refresh and recharge your creative batteries slips away.

After personal time, work starts eating into family time. Missing that one game for the kids. Getting the partner to go to teacher conferences. Putting on a movie after dinner to distract the kids. I know because I've been there, and I regret it!

You and I and everyone else knows this is Not Good. Is this what you'd want to see your children doing? Is this what you want to recommend to your clients for their lifestyle? No. All the tired "give up everything else and focus on your start-up" coaching from the dot-com era doesn't apply for a fulfilling lifestyle.

In order to be fully present, you must be fully recharged. That means time and attention for your inner world, your physical world, and your relationship world. Wholeness. The reason to be **a skilled steward of your own time and attention is to participate actively in generating your next best evolution, for yourself and for the planet.**

So you need to choose when you're available for clients ... and when you're not.

As you grow your team, build generative boundaries into your culture. Discuss what availability needs really are, and whether they have a rhythm (during a launch, for example). Explore how to handle primary and secondary communication channels as a team. Help each team member create and honor their own generative boundaries around the team's work so that their lives remain fulfilling. In your project debrief sessions, openly discuss processes and systems that can avoid crisis management the next time around. Continue to handle exceptions with compassionate communication.

And you need to communicate that to them in the most positive way.

Because not only are you protecting your personal and family life experiences, your clients and team are watching how you do it. You are their model for getting out of rescuer mode. With your behavior, **you are their model and muse for creating a fulfilling life**. You matter that much.

So you can communicate up front your "office hours" and expected completion time on projects. Then, when a request comes in for more of you, you model how to **communicate with compassion** in the moment. Purposetivity is not about making rules for yourself to *always* say "no" or *always* say "yes." It's about tuning in to the moment and the wholeness of Life and answering from a larger perspective.

In addition, you can use tools to manage interruptions and distractions. For example, www.freedom.to coordinates blocks of "off the hook" time across all your devices. We'll be talking about processes that work *your* way to see that things get done with maximum harmony.

Chapter 15
What's Going On?
Supportive Systems

How do you know where you stand and whether you're moving in the direction that's right for you?

How do you track relationships? How do you monitor client progress? How do you manage finances? What are your web tools and assets?

Tracking the elements of delivery and having useful business status information at your fingertips is the reason for **Supportive Systems.**

Your Supportive Systems include the hardware and software (yes, phones, too) on which your technology runs, the cloud-based tools you use, and the processes for how it all fits together to get work done. We don't like to think of people as gears in a system, but often the *work* you ask them to do is.

This is also where you design the processes and tools that **make it all run smoothly so that you can focus on loving your people—** which is the focus of the whole next section of this book!

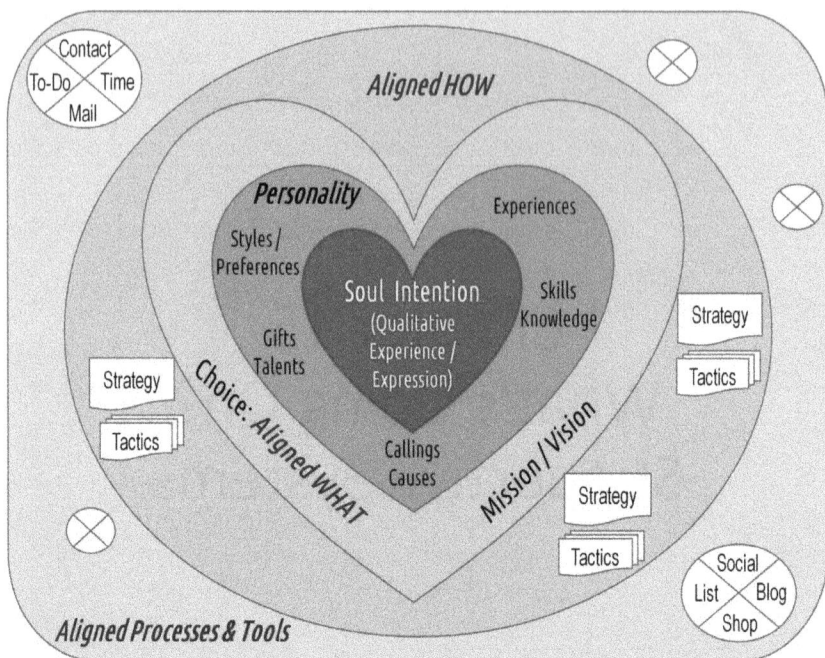

Just as with the other aspects of business, picking up "systems" from a blueprint or just because someone offers a "done for you" package may not support your Purposetivity. Even if they help you to be very efficient—productive—if you're doing the wrong things really, really well ... it doesn't advance your Purpose.

What Needs to Be Tracked?

Review your Succulent Indicators to see what needs to be tracked and determine how you'll monitor each one. Sometimes a simple list or spreadsheet is fine. For other areas, like response rates or accounting, specialized software comes into play.

The whole Action and Automation section of this book fits in this area of your business plan, so you can expect to review the processes that make each Circle of Success run smoothly, the tools that support running them your way, and how to bring your team into the picture.

When you identify the processes that repeat in your business and document how to do them, these documents can make your own life so much easier than figuring out how to do them each time— and certainly contribute to delegation!

Store your process, scripts, templates, and measurement requirements in your "procedures manual," whether that's an online folder of documents or Evernote notebook of pages (or something else). Printed manuals are difficult to share and keep updated when you have team members.

These are the systems that you get to design specifically to support you and your style!

Chapter 16
You Are the Most Important
Resource: Inner Adventures

And in the most cyclical of ways, now we return your attention to your self.

Perhaps the most fulfilling part of owning your own business is the **Inner Adventures!**

In service to this vision and mission, which aspects of your divine self come forward? Which need to recede? It's not about becoming a "new you." It's about emphasizing facets of your diamond that have been there all along!

Unlike the old corporate days, you're not looking for something "wrong" that needs to be addressed like in the old standardized "development plans." Your goal is to support your own **evolution from perfection to perfection**.

What specific areas fascinate you and/or would significantly contribute to your ability to run your business smoothly? Remember that many "important" but distasteful areas of your business are prime areas to hire (contract) someone who already has the expertise—you just have to be able to communicate with them!

Where would you feel excited to extend your skills? In your:

- Craft
- Personal development, habits, and behaviors
- Visioning and planning
- Marketing
- Creativity and development
- Delivery and tracking
- Finances and analytics
- Other

For each one, note the level of training up next for you: beginner, intermediate, advanced.

People who design education programs organize developmental objectives according to Blooms hierarchy. Sometimes a "lightweight" familiarity with material is sufficient. In other cases, you really need to be able to apply what you know to create your outcomes. What level of shift is being called forth?

- Remembering—recognize or recall information
- Understanding—explain ideas or concepts

- Applying—use the information in a new way
- Analyzing—distinguish among different parts, compare, differentiate, discriminate, question, test
- Evaluating—justify a decision, judge, select, support
- Creating—create new product or idea, design, develop
- Transforming—inspire change

Research and ask colleagues where to find the best training in each area, then find out when that training is offered. Plan your calendar—and your budget—to incorporate the self-improvement needed for the highest caliber of leadership.

As you expand your team, this section also expands to include how you consciously create culture and support the growth of every person. We'll cover more of this in Section 3, "Expand and Evolve."

Self-Care for the Leader in You

In addition to regular education, taking exquisite care of the core of your business—you—determines how much YOU have to bring to the table.

Build your biorhythms into your daily plans to keep yourself recharged. Taking, *actually taking!*, vacations and time off is crucial to recharge and reflect.

Look at how you are nourished on every level:

- Body (food, movement, temperature, environment)
- Heart (solitude, friends, nature)
- Mind (reading, learning, creating, discussing)
- Soul (prayer or meditation, journaling, art, nature)

Build it all into your plan. It's all YOURS! You can build a sacred space in your office and light a candle while you work if you like. You can have various kinds of background music available. How about a mini-fridge stocked with top-quality nutrition for your day? You can open up floor space for stretching or put in a couch for stretching out. Naps rock!

Especially if you are a service-based professional (coach, healer, therapist), how will you know when you are walking your own talk?

Chapter 17
Non-Linear Business Spirals

Remember that developing your business plan is a spiral. It evolves continuously based on your life cycle of express, listen, adapt, and respond. As with skiing, steering adjustments are **always easier when you're already in motion**.

Now that you've had a chance to get to know each Circle of Success and the business contribution it represents, revisit each section of your business plan and note:

- How would you phrase the goal of that area contributing to success on your own terms?
- What challenges does it present for you? What do you have to be able to do or grow into?
- What does it mean to do it in alignment with your vision?
- What is your process to prototype and adapt? When will you review and adjust?
- What skills/resources do you already have?
- What beliefs hold you back?
- How will you FEEL when it is flowing in alignment?

And when you have fully embodied this stage of success, you can look to upleveling to the next stage of business development.

Overlap and Integration

The areas of business planning are interrelated, of course. That's why the circles overlap in our picture. Revisit each area to see what notes you want to make from that into related areas.

From Inspired Vision

- How often do you want to review your vision? (Make notes in Supportive Systems.)
- What is your process to adapt your vision as you evolve? (Make notes in Supportive Systems.)
- What skills do you already have? What skills do you need to articulate your vision? (Make notes in Inner Adventures.)
- What beliefs hold you back? (Make notes in Inner Adventures.)

From Succulent Indicators

- What knowledge/skills do you need grow (or hire) to track your indicators? (Make notes in Inner Adventures.)
- How often do you want to review your indicators? (Make notes in Supportive Systems.)
- What tools do you need to track your indicators? (Make notes in Supportive Systems.)
- What is your process to adapt your indicators as you evolve? (Make notes in Supportive Systems.)
- Does this collection of indicators feel aligned with your business vision?

From Joyful Communications

- Identify indicators to carry to Succulent Indicators.
- Identify personal and professional development opportunities for Inner Adventures.

- Note all the things you get to create in your Exuberant Creativity section.
- Identify Supportive Systems requirements.

From Exuberant Creativity

- Identify indicators to carry to Succulent Indicators.
- Identify development opportunities to add to Inner Adventures.
- Identify Supportive Systems requirements.

From Celebrating Delivery

- Identify indicators to carry to Succulent Indicators.
- Verify congruence with Inspired Vision.
- Identify Inner Adventures development opportunities.
- Identify Supportive Systems requirements. What tools and processes do you need to keep track of this?

From Inner Adventures

- Identify indicators to carry to Succulent Indicators.
- Verify congruence with Inspired Vision.
- Identify Supportive Systems requirements.

Bridging

"But what if I am in a job I hate? Doing what I love won't pay the bills tomorrow."

Trace the job back to why you have it—providing food, shelter, basics. Find the qualitative word that describes that level of experience (many on the planet don't have even that). Is it *comfort*? *Safety*?

Knowing the *quality* a job provides, look at the other *qualities* you'd like to be experiencing, and see if you can bring more into your days. Competence. Compassion. Challenge. Creativity.

Second, see **your current situation as a brilliant bridge to your next best future**.

And if you don't currently have a bridge, it can be a totally honorable step to build a financial bridge to what you do want to be experiencing.

Tie Activities Back to Your Mission

One of the advantages that makes Purposetivity so much more engaging than the old productivity systems is your direct line of sight from the task at hand (which may not always be pleasant in itself) to the very deepest, connected reason for doing it. **Every bit of your daily doing flows from your soul's intention** to create a quality of experience in your life, integrated with how you're best suited to accept it.

When you gather your daily "short list" of high-impact tasks, take a few extra seconds to reflect on how that list reflects the wholistic lifestyle your heart desires.

If at any time during the day you start to have that "do I gotta?" feeling, check in to ensure what you're looking at really does connect and support your mission and vision for life.

Chapter 18
Phased Implementation
Is the Path with Joy

Here's where it comes together. You've looked at your style and you've looked at the business model/strategy you want to build out to enjoy. Now make sure the quality of the journey matches the quality of the destination. You want to have your style honored along the way so that DOing business feels good! **Business as a force for good starts in your own heart**. And head. And hands.

We're not talking about setting up an arbitrary five-year goal and embarking on a death march to force your way to it. Quite the opposite! **The feminine approach in Purposetivity emerges organically**. Based on a deep *attunement* to where you are right now and what your soul wants to express and experience, what is your next horizon? Or just your next step?

When our body creates a new human, the trimesters go in a certain order. The development isn't *supposed* to land at the end point before we've begun! **Purposeful business expands with a rhythm, in cycles**.

Build your services out in waves, **like ripples reaching out from your heart**. Start with people nearest you as you learn what resonates. Then you can amplify that rhythm to expand your reach and your impact in the world.

Build your marketing outreach the same way. Rather than trying to put everything in place before you launch (you can't do everything first, remember?), start with "seed launch" to practice your message and your delivery. Find what excites you—and connects with the people you want to play with—then do more of that.

The same "prototype and adapt" philosophy holds for your operational tools and financial tracking. You can start with MailChimp (free), then grow to AWebber long before you need to invest (monthly!) in InfusionSoft. You can start with Evernote and grow to Google tools long before you need to manage team project interactions through Asana. Start with personal checks and grow to PayPal long before you need a full e-commerce website.

Don't be afraid to experiment. All great entrepreneurs do! Try different things. Reach beyond your current comfort zone. You may be surprised! Recognize that a necessary by-product of experimentation is **learning what doesn't work for you**. The quicker you can learn with minimal time and money invested (start small, use trial periods), the better off your bottom line will be as you **move toward the solutions that DO work** for you.

Recommendations and experts can offer great input when it comes to making choices, but keep in mind that you are unique, with a unique combination of style and gifts. What a detail-oriented analytical left-brainer loves and awards five stars may be wonderful, but it may not fit a flowing, wholistic, connection-based businesswoman.

However, you can't build everything first. You don't have to have everything in place before you're "ready." You grow into it. The question is, in what order should the expansion come? Your **phased implementation plan** is your road map that **optimizes your path of evolution** based on getting you into cash flow as early as possible.

Psychology of Flow

One of the most rewarding experiences you can have of yourself is that of flow. When we are "in the flow," we lose sense of time and self and become immersed in the activity. We *are* our attention and actions, with no second-guessing or mental mediation. Athletes and artists talk about getting into their groove, being in the zone. Mihály Csíkszentmihályi, the founding researcher of the experience of flow, discovered that this experience is so fulfilling that people will pursue it beyond any other form of motivation.

The inner experience of flow defines the most vibrant, vivid, exhilarating version of living inspired passion in the moment. When you're in the flow, without resistance, you're a gift to everyone around you. **Your natural contribution flows into the world joyfully**, and it's learnable, teachable, doable. In this book you are seeing precisely how to set up your business vision and milestones, define your own terms of success, and identify exactly what you want to become more skilled at!

So how do you set yourself up to maximize this joy?

You need to have:

- A well-defined goal, desired outcome, vision
- Quick feedback on your progress
- Challenging activity level and matching belief that your skill level can stretch there

The other criteria for you to truly experience flow is freedom from distractions and interruptions.

Go to **www.PurposeDrivenProcess/vaready/lgm-free-gift** *to get my free e-book "7 Simple and Easy Tools to Improve Focus and Flow in Your Business" to remove distractions from your creative time.*

Let's look a bit more at that third item. That *perception* of a match between your skills and the challenge at hand—that it IS achievable—is central because it implies you know what you want to do and how well things are going.

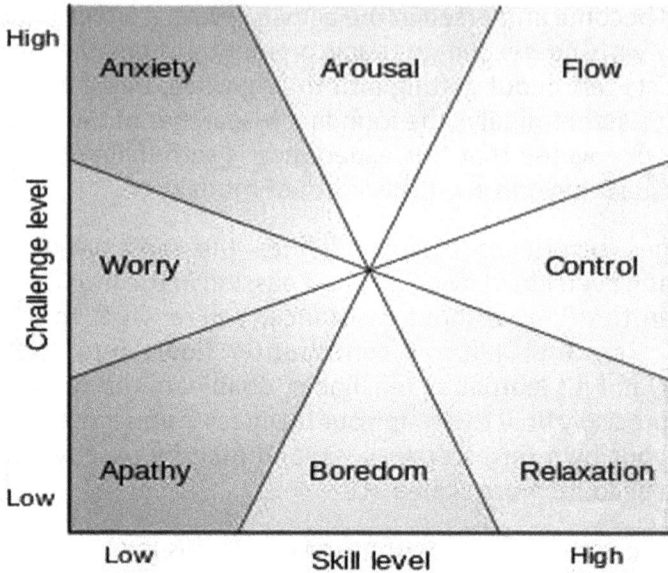

This simple diagram of the interaction between how challenging the task *looks* and how skilled you *think* you are shows how your experience gets created. Notice especially the center of the Challenge band: Worry and Control. These are two of the greatest energy leaks for a business owner!

Now we're going to address how to get a handle on knowing where you stand so that you can relax, neither worrying about what's not in place nor micromanaging to try to overcontrol everything.

Digital Asset Inventory

Each thing you have created reflects a part of you and your mission. Elements, or whole items, can be repurposed to support what you are currently building—if you don't forget you even have them! Just like fashions, different elements tend to return to favor in cycles. (Women get this!)

Making a list of your creations—images, words, information flow— helps you review what you can reuse to support each new project.

What do you already have in place?

How well does it match the quality of experience you're creating for yourself and your clients (and your branding)?

Fill in the box with the location of the asset, not just an X.

	Missing	Needs Updates	Just Right (for now)	Location
Business card				
Signature talk				
Handouts and worksheets from talks				
Brochure layout, flyers				
Other talks you've given (outline, script, slides—whatever!)				
Bio (short and long form)				
Headshot				
Other photos of you or your work				
Credibility website				
Sales website				
Blog posts				
Articles you've written				
Social media presence				
"What do you do" statement				
Testimonials				
Opt-in gifts and giveaways				
Workshop or retreat agendas				
Autoresponder text				
Info product				
Recordings and interviews				
Notes from training or education				
Press release copy				
Former website copy				
Letterhead and slide templates				
Questionnaires, intake forms, and assessments you do for other coaches				
Contracts, agreements, and progress report forms				

Here's a bonus idea: when you have a really great journal rant about your business, use your smart phone to go into Evernote and capture a picture of it. It's very quick to do and it becomes searchable!

The next category of digital assets are the tools you already have in place and operational. Even if you have implemented some strategies before you're really ready, it's good to know where you stand.

Fill in the proper box with the name of your tool rather than just an X.

	Missing	Needs Updates	Just Right (for now)	Location
Operating system (Mac or PC)				
E-mail folders				
Contact list with e-mails and phone numbers together				
Calendar				
To-do list				
Web browser				
Notes and research				
Opt-in / autoresponder system				
Website				
Shopping cart				
Merchant account				
Give webinars				
Remote sessions/meetings				
Social media				
Personal contact relationship manager (not the opt-in program) for clients and prospecting				
Travel management				
Event logistics				
Slide presentation				
Screen captures				
e-book development and delivery				
Audio recording				
Membership site				
File sharing				
Client session notes				
Antivirus				
Password locker				
Backup management				
Team project management & communication				
Bookkeeping				
Receipts				
Mileage				

Not everyone needs everything, and you don't need everything first! This is just to be very clear on where you stand today.

Order Steps by Cash Flow

Compare your diagram for your ideal business design from the previous section with your asset inventory. Mark the key items that you need to get in place for your design to work. **Remember that you don't have to do everything first!**

As you go through this process, be open to recognizing the "Voice of Should" in your head: what experts say you "should" have in place; family expectations for what you "should" be doing or earning; social media memes about how your kind of business "should" look. These social norms are common, and we all carry the virus. Each time you discover one, jot it down and return your attention to YOUR why, YOUR style, and YOUR big picture. We're looking to discover your unique "how," the way that is just perfect for you to experience the quality of business and life your heart and soul desire.

Start Small and Build It Out to Match Your Desired Lifestyle

You don't want to have one of everything. And you certainly don't need everything "first." Revisit your ideal Big Picture to see where you want to end up. If someone offers you a strategy that doesn't match, you know it's a Shiny Bright Object and give it a pass, at least for now.

Create a safe page in your business plan for "Future Opportunities," or you can simply call it "Not Now." Today you'll only look at the top or "now" areas and plan those out. For the rest, repeat, "I don't need to know that yet."

And remember: You don't need everything in place before you begin. There are people LOOKING for you right now. Just **put yourself in their way!**

Service Business Pathway

If you want to build an in-person service (one-to-one or group, local or online) business, start with directness.

There are no immediate clients in your home office.

People first, live, in-person

Go where the people are. Meetup.com is your friend. Listen. Practice your offer. MAKE offers. Invite people to find out more, and invite them to work with you. Gather trends and testimonials.

Make sure they can find you again. Have a business card. Have a website with contact info, just for credibility. Adding "value" to your site can come later.

Web presence

Once you know what works in terms of describing how you make a difference, take those words to your website. Your first website only needs to back up your credibility. Just one page will do, so long as it has a picture of you, some description of the results you provide your clients, **and your contact information**.

When you start to expand it, create a simple gift (poster or e-book list) and start collecting names so that you can invite people to your offerings in the future. If they like what you're doing now, they'll want to stay informed. Make that easy on both of you!

Extend your web presence into social media. Know whether your ideal clients hang out on Facebook, LinkedIn, Twitter, Instagram, etc. Become active in group discussions.

As you grow, you can expand your website to have multiple pages—even a blog if you love to write (or video log or photo blog or podcast or ...).

Finally, when you have information products to sell, you will need to add e-commerce to it.

Suggested reading: *Rich Dad, Poor Dad* to learn about the importance of cash flow.

Product Business Pathway

If you want to build a manufacturing (recordings or invention or crafts) business, you need online access (e-commerce) and searchability. Yes, you can start with some local sales, but it isn't going to build large enough to be self-sustaining until your widget is available for online orders.

Your Expansion Roadmap

Now look at what you want to build and highlight the things you actually need. Just don't highlight the "overachievement" things from earlier plans.

In your Big Picture, **what is the step that could introduce someone to your work fastest**? Getting into **positive cash flow** is generally the first priority. It could be as easy as printing some simplified business cards just so that people have your phone number and e-mail address so that they CAN find you again. Or it may be to attend local gatherings to test what messages resonate with people before building out your website.

A. List the first thing, the real first thing, that can **directly affect your bottom line**. You're probably looking at something you can begin this week. How will you recognize that it's done?

B. When that's done, what will be the next phase? This may be something you can get done in the coming month. How will you recognize that it's done?

C. What seems like it would be the phase after that? When you start to look out three to six months, you need to leave more room for adaptation. You can't know yet because part of what you do earlier is to gather information. So here you're sketching the most likely ripples of expansion, without setting your heart on them too much.

Now Put It into Your Calendar

Get an annual calendar for planning if you don't already have one.

Put the key end results (how you'd recognize that it's done) on the calendar. Verify to yourself this is a SMART goal—specific, measurable, achievable, relevant ... and on the calendar timely!

Take the pieces one at a time, first one first. What steps do you need to take to make that happen? Sketch those timelines on your calendar. When it looks realistic, copy the items into your task manager.

Then proceed to the next phase and identify the steps and get them down to be done AFTER the others. Part of the magic of laying it all out this way is **you don't have to try to do everything at once AND you know nothing is getting lost** or dropped. The system provides reassurance to back up your self-trust.

Every single thing you're entering is DIRECTLY related to you building exactly the business experience you want to have. This matters!

This Is Not the End

You may want to add many pieces to your business puzzle, but keep your initial flow simple. Once you have these pieces in place and reliably, sustainably bringing you client business, then you can look toward your next creative evolution and how you would most enjoy expanding horizons.

When your transformation involves helping people be more authentic, don't put on airs about where you are in your business. Every business goes through growth stages, and your tools and presentation can be effective and **perfectly matched to the stage you're currently growing through**.

There was a time when home-based businesses had to hide the fact to try to appear more professional and credible. But these days, we are the majority—and often what the rest wish they could be doing! Your systems need to work to let people do business with you. And as much as possible, they need to do so quietly, without taking attention from you or your client. Over time, you can upgrade pieces as you need to for more capacity or capabilities.

Section 2
Action and Automation

Chapter 19
Benefits of Automation

AFTER you know who you are and what you want to build that's going to feel right to you and support the lifestyle you actually want to experience, processes and tools help you **automate the mechanics so that you can focus on what matters most—being fully present with your people**.

I understand that most of the big corporations were built in the days of paper planners. Not having fully recovered from my personal addiction to paper planner systems, I more than understand the enjoyment of the feel of pen on paper,

Yet consider the context in which those paper planners were sufficient. Take, for example, an insurance salesperson in the 1970s.

- Learn the skills of a sales conversation and learn your company's products.
- Identify prospects to call on. Participate in golf and charities.
- List them in your planner.
- Block the time to make calls.

- Schedule resulting appointments in your planner. (Executives had secretaries for this.)
- Meet with the prospect to determine fit.
- Complete contracts if appropriate.
- Add to annual checkup list.
- Prepare monthly status report for management.

Now Compare That with Today

- Learn the skills of a sales conversation and learn your company's products.
- Create a marketing plan to become known in your field.
- Invest in website development.
  - Learn all social media tools
- Identify prospects to call on. Participate in golf and charities.
- List them in your planner.
  - Rarely listing cold calls now. List activities to create pull marketing.
  - Blog and post regularly to be visible.
  - Network with local referral sources.
  - Watch Meet Up for opportunities.
- Block the time to make calls.
  - Make calls between chauffeuring children to activities because both spouses work.
  - Make calls between chauffeuring your aging parent to medical appointments.
  - Balance in-person and online (Skype) meetings.
  - Adapt schedule daily to high-priority interruptions.
  - Field back-and-forth of e-mail and texts and instant messages.
  - Add giving talks and free seminars to get people intrigued to call you.
- Schedule resulting appointments in your planner, coordinating online calendars.

- o Reschedule when the prospect has anything else come up.
- o Clients text with immediate requests whenever they think of it.
- Meet with the prospect to determine fit.
- Complete contracts if appropriate.
  - o Follow up e-mail and more forms.
  - o Follow on social media to stay engaged.
- Add to annual checkup list.
- Prepare monthly status report for management.
  - o When the cloud servers are up.
  - o Daily motivational meeting takes your key time.

The higher demands of always-on availability and connectivity, as well as a much more educated population through the internet, significantly shift the demands on your time. Rather than each day being more or less similar, now **wildly different requirements show up at any moment**. No two days are the same.

How can you set up a routine?

You can't.

That's one of the big reasons why **old-fashioned productivity systems don't cut the mustard anymore**. The world has changed. People's expectations have changed. YOUR expectations have changed!

That paper planner that worked so well? Where are you going to also insert your blog calendar? Random things people ask you to do? Who has time to write out a to-do list, then copy 80% of it over again tomorrow? And people's phone numbers and e-mail addresses? **And how will you share this information with team members if it's on paper?**

Oh, sure, you're going to block off time for yourself. And as soon as your adorable kid needs you, you're there. When a client calls with an emergency—that's exactly the block you'll fit the work into. **Paper planners can't keep up with today's complexities.**

My suggestion is to split out your inspirational morning journaling and do that in a perfect paper book, with a wonderful pen.

And **put all your personal and business management into the computer, which is really good at remembering and organizing things!**

Why Automate?

Bottom line, you have three key reasons to automate your toolset:

1. Location independence
2. Sharable, delegatable (especially remote)
3. Peace of mind

This is one of your key strategies in shifting from mere productivity to Purposetivity. Eliminate mechanical rework and **free your attention** for what matters!

Location Independence

Consider a coach whose practice is mostly full. She wants to go overseas for a month to take a class, tour, and be able to work while she's there.

How many paper client files does she need to haul around?

Woe be the day when you leave your paper planner at home. Or in the car. Or at the doctor's office and they're closed for the weekend! Everything you need to do for ANYthing is in that book, and there's only one way to access it—hold it in your hands.

With the proper tools, the information you need is available wherever you are. At a networking meeting and you want to set up a follow-up coffee? Pull out your phone and put it in your calendar.

At the office and reading e-mail on your computer when you get a meeting request? Open the calendar window on your computer and put it in there.

The same information is available and synchronized (automatically) across all your access devices.

How about the notes for that talk you're developing? If you leave the pad of paper at home when you head off on a trip, you pretty much have to start over to get anything done. By collecting your research references and sketches and ideas as they come to you in an automated tool like Evernote, you can do most of the work on your big-screen computer, add notes from your phone in moments of inspiration, and still share the notebook with your editor.

Which brings us to the second benefit of automation:

Sharable, Delegatable Tasks and Information

How will a virtual assistant (VA) be able to add client appointments to your paper calendar if you're carrying it around? Are you going to go home every night and copy new entries into the online shared calendar? (No, and you know it!)

To be able to offload the tasks you like least, you need to be able to provide access to the information and tools for the person to be successful. You can't hoard the information with you on the cruise ship.

Not only does this mean putting the information in the computer, it means ensuring the tool you select supports sharing. A calendar or contact system that resides on your hard disk is accessible only by you (unless you leave the system always on and have your VA remote into your whole system!). The tools you select need to support remote synchronization or be cloud-based.

Because when your assistant is hugely successful in supporting you, you get ...

Peace of Mind

Computers remember things really well. I don't.

Computers help me search across lots of storage quickly. Spiral binders don't.

Computers make it possible for someone else to get in there and handle the details.

'Nuff said.

Automation Empowers Your Values

Think about the top values you bring to your business. When you want more than just a job's income, you want meaning and significance. You want to make a difference with people. You need to **reclaim your full attention from menial tasks** to be present with the people you care about.

When you want to make a larger impact in the world than one person can make, you need to be able to share the work and collaborate on outcomes.

When you want freedom and autonomy, you need to be able to **let the computer do what it does best so that you can do what you do best.**

When you want to travel and continue to serve, when you want people to have access to your expertise around the clock without your intervention, online tools support you fully.

When you become the master of your technology, you control your time and attention; it doesn't control you!

Automation gives you the foundation for those values and lifestyle choices to come true.

Chapter 20
Phases and Flows

If you would like more detailed steps for this section, check out my online course, "VA Ready in 60 Days or Less."

One of the best ways to think about jobs you want to automate or delegate is how their repetition flows. While each flower is unique, they all start from buds. By articulating—making conscious—the phases in the life cycle of that job, you make all your communication around it clearer.

Also, while one flower may be in full bloom, another right next to it may just be budding out, while another may be going to seed. Tracking a variety of instances as they pass through the same phases is how you stay organized and confident.

While a flower is in one phase, a transformation occurs that **moves it to the next phase**. Some transformations involve external elements; others are based on internal growth or change. So we'll be thinking of your business process in terms of **phase (describe it) then transform (what changes and what empowers those**

changes), then next phase and next transform, and so on through the natural life cycle of the process.

Strawberry Fields Forever

Let's look at the phases a strawberry goes through to see how this plays out.

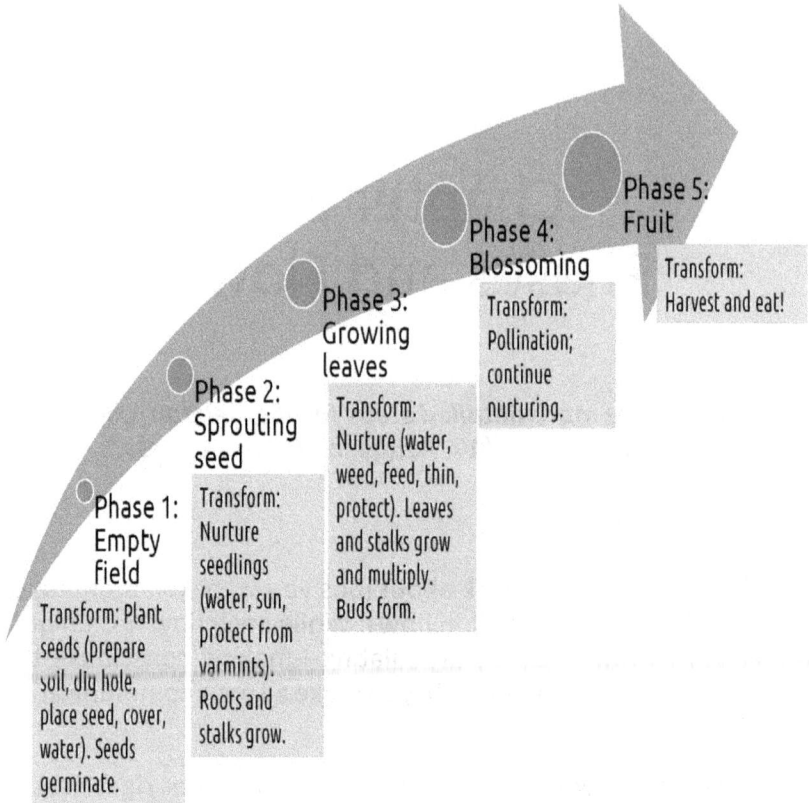

Phase 5: Fruit
Transform: Harvest and eat!

Phase 4: Blossoming
Transform: Pollination; continue nurturing.

Phase 3: Growing leaves
Transform: Nurture (water, weed, feed, thin, protect). Leaves and stalks grow and multiply. Buds form.

Phase 2: Sprouting seed
Transform: Nurture seedlings (water, sun, protect from varmints). Roots and stalks grow.

Phase 1: Empty field
Transform: Plant seeds (prepare soil, dig hole, place seed, cover, water). Seeds germinate.

Of course, we could divide this into an arbitrary number of phases (and real farmers do!). But for most of the business processes with which you'll be working, three to seven is a good range to manage.

So How Does This Translate to a Business Process?

Consider the process a prospect goes through from finding out about you to actually working with you.

Phase 1: "Empty field." The person has not ever experienced you before. You may be speaking to a group or networking or waiting for an oil change. One way or another, a conversation opens up, and you plant the seed that the person may be interested in finding out about your work. You make sure they can find you again (business card or a handout with notes from your talk), perhaps get their contact information, and that seed is germinating.

Phase 2: "Sprouting seed." The person is aware of you and interested enough to go check out your website, which nurtures them with value and a gift. They may sign up for your newsletter or follow you on social media.

Phase 3: "Growing leaves." As they become more comfortable with your voice and style, they begin to evaluate whether they'd like to actually work with you. They see the social proof and become personally interested in the results you describe.

Phase 4: "Blossoming." Through whatever channel, the person reaches out to set up an appointment to talk with you. You nurture them through your consultation session, determine which mode of interaction is the best fit for the two of you, and provide them an offer.

Phase 5: "Fruit." They are excited to begin your program and enroll. They are now a client and that is a phase in a different process!

Phase 0: "Fallow." Anywhere along the way, a prospect may determine you are not a match at this time and return to fallow ground. They may return someday. They may send friends. But for now, no effort is required from you.

How Does This Relate to Delegation?

In looking toward automating—and delegating!—those tasks that feel like "overhead" and take our time and attention, we have to be able to describe what we're doing to be able to teach someone else. Often we're either in a zone of **unconscious competence**, doing it so naturally it's hard to slow down and talk *about* it, or **very conscious incompetence**, detesting and avoiding then just slamming through in a panic to get something done, which is not what we want our assistant to do!

Getting familiar with the concepts of life cycles and work flows makes delegation a lot easier. (Note that different tools use different terms for these concepts, so you may have to translate a bit as you put things in place.)

Defining Process Phases

Many of the things we work with go through a **defined sequence of phases**, which are generally not actually called "germinating" and "blossoming."

For more clarity in context, we use more descriptive words. In sales prospecting and enrolling, someone we talk to is "Aware" of our services, then "Evaluates" the match, has been "Offered" a package, becomes a "Client," or says "No."

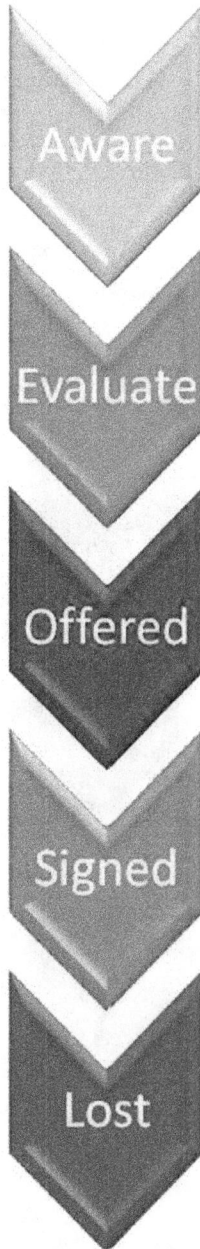

Aware

Evaluate

Offered

Signed

Lost

In a different example, during development, a product (event/info product/etc.) you want to build starts out as an idea, then you work on the "Requirements," begin the "Design," actually "Develop" it, "Test" it, "Deliver" it, and "Archive" it.

How Do Work Flows Fit In?

For each phase of the process, we typically have a set of tasks we "always" do at that stage of the game. Except when we forget.

A work flow defines the **collection of all the tasks, in order**, that we would like to do for a given phase.

So when we sign a new client, we might want to:

1. Get payment.

2. Collect all contact information.

3. Provide them an agreement to sign.

4. Receive signed agreement.

5. Set up our client note and tracking system for them.

6. Thank the person who referred them.

7. Move their record into the "Signed" phase.

Sometimes the new client wasn't referred, so we can delete that task in this instance. But it's good to have a "master list" so that nothing falls through the cracks.

Here's a sample prospecting work flow.

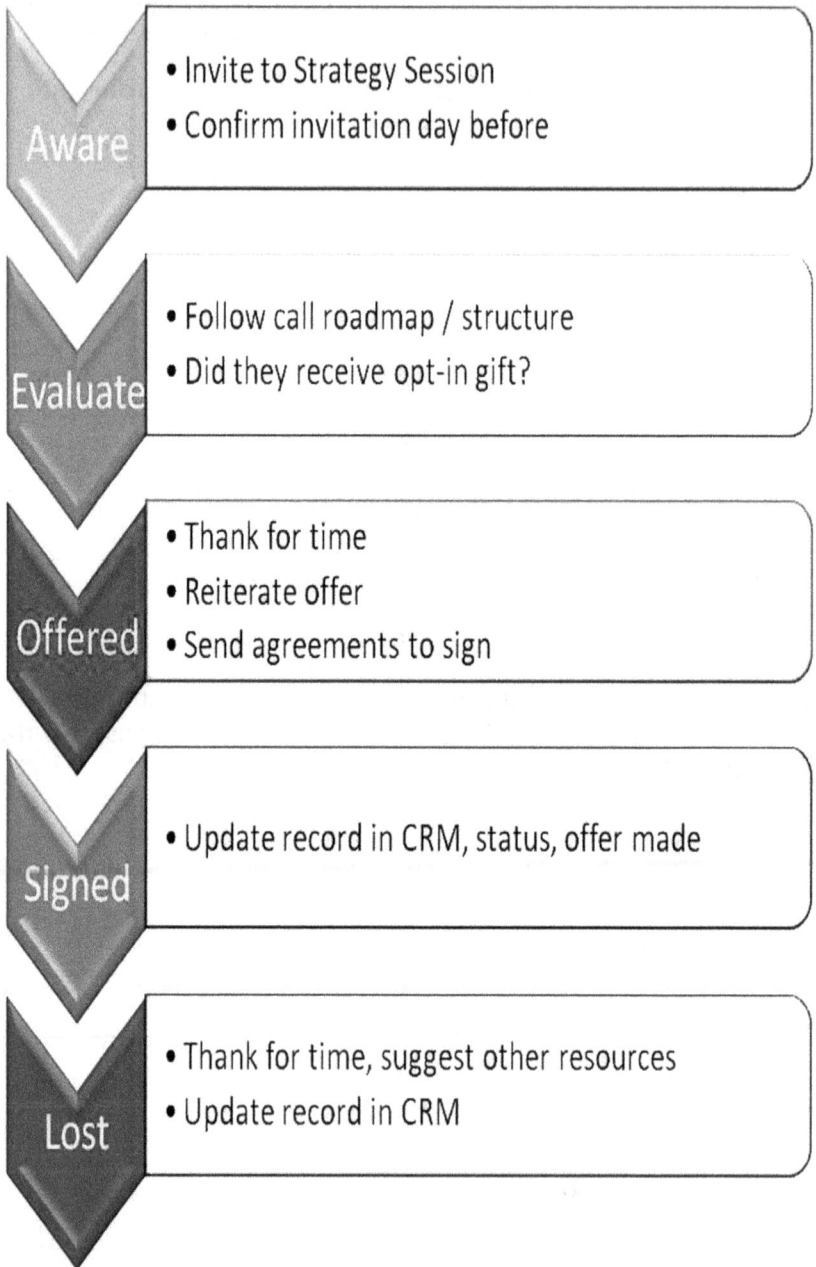

Aware
- Invite to Strategy Session
- Confirm invitation day before

Evaluate
- Follow call roadmap / structure
- Did they receive opt-in gift?

Offered
- Thank for time
- Reiterate offer
- Send agreements to sign

Signed
- Update record in CRM, status, offer made

Lost
- Thank for time, suggest other resources
- Update record in CRM

For You to Do

Now it's time for you to identify the processes that repeat in your business. These can be the first ones you automate—or delegate!

The goal is to set up a repeatable, RELATIVE mapping (delivery minus 3 months ... delivery minus three weeks ... delivery minus three days) that shows you the dependencies and lead times for milestones and deliverables. This "treasure map" becomes the template for you to delegate to team members.

Choose a Process

First, identify areas where something in your business goes through a series of phases. Areas to consider (pick one to learn on):

- Prospect tracking
- Client status (progression through program)
- Requesting a speaking opportunity (much like prospecting)
- Paying and recording a bill that arrives
- Developing a new program
- Coordinating a marketing launch
- Running a group call or hosting a live group event
- Taking an educational class
- Areas from your personal life (menu planning and shopping)
- Developing a blog post

Business area process I'm working with first:

_____

What is the thing I'm tracking? (person, launch, post, program, etc.)

Name Your Phases

Name the phases of the life cycle. Usually a person or project or whatever type of item you're tracking goes through three to seven distinct phases from brand new to completed. Identify the phases for your process here. (You may not need all seven spaces.)

Phase 1:

Phase 2:

Phase 3:

Phase 4:

Phase 5:

Phase 6:

Phase 7:

In addition, identify **how you know** when it "enters" and "exits" each phase.

Identify the Steps

Now "look inside" each of those phases you named. When you mentally open that box, jot down **every task** you can think of that "should" get done in that phase to **assist the process to move to the next phase**. Even if no actual flow uses *all* of them, it's great to have a master list! You may want to put the tasks on sticky notes so that you can arrange them and move things around. You'll want to mark which ones depend on others or which ones can't start until something else gets done.

This would make a great notebook for you to set up in Evernote, with a note for each phase. You could also use a folder of documents to hold these so that you can have more flexibility than I can print here in a book.

Once you get your project and task management system set up (upcoming chapter), you can enter the whole process as a template to copy and repeat.

When you start mapping these to this year's calendar, watch for overlap between projects. **Honor the lifestyle you're creating.**

Document Everything You Touch

Here's a key to making this whole investment much less costly: every time you go in to "do" something in your business, start documenting your steps.

First, and especially for things you do only occasionally, it means you don't have to remember the steps or figure them out again every time you return. You're creating your own task-based manuals—not everything that could be done, but how to get done the specific thing you want done!

Second, these documents form the foundation of the procedures when you bring your team on board. We'll discuss that more later.

Finally, and something I realized only recently, if I were to get hit by a bus, these procedures would allow my children to continue the business income stream.

Processes to start capturing:

- Blog posting
- Autoresponder creation and sequencing
- Bookkeeping
- Social media (even if it's just your philosophy for now)
- Lead processing and prospecting (what you do with business cards)
- Client session notes and recordings
- Speaking engagements
- Event checklists

For now, invest in a screen capture program (print screen will do; I like SnagIt).

Make your numbered list of steps in a document or an Evernote notebook. Use the image tool to circle where to look on the screen (in the current version anyway) at each step.

It's a great (GREAT!) start, and it just piggybacks onto stuff you're doing anyway right now.

Chapter 21
Tools That Fit

Cramming yourself into tools that don't suit your personality is no more fun than walking in high-heeled shoes that don't fit your feet! You get wobbles and blisters and are reluctant to take the next step.

Bringing all of who you are to the table lets you evaluate which tools support you in **experiencing the business you want to enjoy running**. This is totally about the quality of the journey!

Notice that the way we've set this up, your "Why" and your "What" are already in place. You definitely don't want build the wrong thing really quickly, so **first make sure what you're doing is On Purpose**. Effective.

Then look to how to make it efficient and fun. This is the "How."

See the difference between traditional productivity and Purposetivity? There's no point being highly productive, producing lots and lots, if you're not On Purpose. Hating the "How" leads to burnout! Your tools have to fit YOUR hands!

What Tools Do I Need? The Tool Temple

Your gift package includes a temple diagram for you to write on, as well as a worksheet of tool requirements per stage that you can fill in yourself.

Each area of your business plan calls for specific types of tools, yet there are some overlaps across all areas (like e-mail!). Having listed all the tools by business area and then gathered them by the job they perform, here is a way for you to see how the tools fit together:

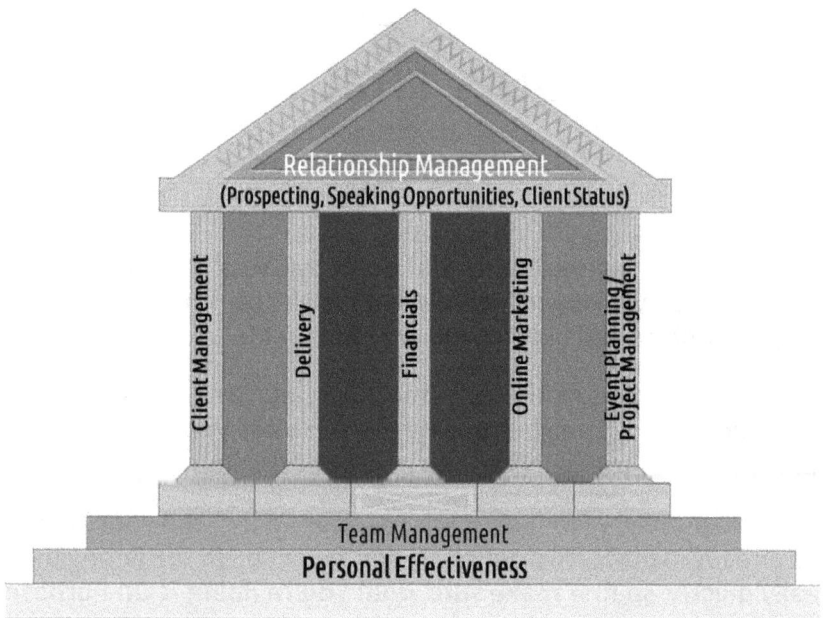

Relationship Management
(Prospecting, Speaking Opportunities, Client Status)

Client Management | Delivery | Financials | Online Marketing | Event Planning / Project Management

Team Management
Personal Effectiveness

Foundation

Personal effectiveness is the foundation of your tool set. Until you can rely on yourself and have access to your information without having to store it all in your head, you can't build reliable relationships with clients or partners.

The elements of this foundation include your e-mail, to-do list, calendar, contacts, notes/research, browser, passwords, and backup programs. You'll also want some miscellaneous tools, especially on your phone, like a calculator, flashlight, recorder, screen capture, and voice to text. Some of my favorite web browser programs are Adblocker, omwriter, asoftmurmur.com, Facebook purity, and freedom.to.

Vertical Pillars

Beyond the basics, the collection of tools for your business depends on how you've matched your business to your style. A local networking-based business requires relatively simple tools compared with internet marketing. Whatever strategy or business model you connect with, the **right tools make it run more smoothly** and enable you to delegate more!

Client management tools enable you to track session notes, programs signed up for, payment dates, and sessions remaining. For the most part, these are for your internal business process management.

Delivery tools, on the other hand, cover how you share your expertise with clients. This could be with designing slides, providing recordings, membership sites or groups, and audio/video webcast delivery.

Financial management tools are the basic bookkeeping, payment merchant account, expenses and receipts, mileage tracking, and status reports. You may want to discuss this with your CPA and/or bookkeeper to know which tools best facilitate interaction as well as give you a picture of how you're doing.

Online marketing covers the popular process of using an opt-in form to gather a list of e-mails, send automatic nurturing messages, offer products and programs, and an online e-commerce or shopping cart site for purchases without your direct involvement.

Event planning/Project management tools track all the logistics, locations, registrations, scheduling, vendors, etc. involved in hosting a live event or delivering an extended project with many parts and players.

Capstone

Where your contact management tool at the foundation level contains names, e-mail addresses, phone numbers, and data, **relationship management** helps you follow up and remember content. What did you last talk about? What were their chief concerns? When did you agree to call them back? A contact relationship management (CRM) package is far more than a list of e-mail addresses in your Google contact list. You can use it for prospecting, client status, and tracking speaking and marketing launches.

One Tool with Multiple Jobs

Depending on your personal style assessment, you may lean toward finding the ideal tool for each area or having one generalized tool that you make do enough for you.

Having fewer interfaces to learn (and teach team members) has a lot of benefits, especially if you're not technically inclined. However, it often means going through an extra step or two to bend the tool to suit you.

This book will use Evernote as the demo tool since it's the most versatile; however you may want to use a specific tool with a better fit. Evernote is like driving a mini-van. It does a whole lot of things pretty darn well, yet a pickup would be able to haul more, a sports car could do better in turns, and a hybrid could get better gas mileage. But for overall utility, our mini-van is Evernote.

Only Learn the 20% You Need to Start on Each Tool

Don't fall in love with the tool for the tool's sake (that's my job). As you configure and "move in," learn the key features needed to support the work you want to get done. By focusing on the portion that supports your purpose, you save the time you would spend (and prevent yourself from getting overwhelmed) trying to read the entire *For Dummies* series. You don't have time for that!

Computer geeks use the acronym CRUD. Learn enough to be able to Create, Read, Update, and Delete each type of item and you're good.

When you bring on team members, they'll only need this task-specific training as well.

Various Tools to Consider

New tools get invented and improvements get delivered way faster than I could keep up with in a printed book. Check my website for my current favorites in each category, and expect to take these as hints for you to look more deeply into the ones that appear interesting.

	More left brain / list oriented	More right brain / visual	Advanced business stages
Basic Productivity			
E-mail	IQTell Outlook Thunderbird GMX	Gmail Apple Inky	
Calendar	Outlook	Google Apple	TimeTrade ScheduleOnce Calendly
Contact	Insightly		
Tasks	IQTell Evernote TargetProcess3 Todoist	Trello DigiSpoke Creately Casual	Asana Teamwork Podio
Notes / Research	Evernote	Evernote Pocket	
Security	Avast, Norton, McAfee LastPass	MalwareBytes DashLane	

	More left brain / list oriented	More right brain / visual	Advanced business stages
Client Management			
Session notes			
Program enrollment / completion			
Delivery / Development			
Slides		PowerPoint	
Membership	WordPress password	FB Group	Kajabi CustomerHub Mimbarium
Writing (book)	MSWord		
Recording (audio/video)	Audacity		
Sessions / Recordings	InstantTeleseminar	Skype, Zoom EasyWebinar Google Hangout	GoToWebinar MaestroConference
File sharing	GoogleDrive, Box	DropBox	

	More left brain / list oriented	More right brain / visual	Advanced business stages
Financials			
Bookkeeping	QuickBooks	Quicken Mint	QuickBooks
Payment / merchant	WooCommerce	Square PayPal	InfusionSoft Ontraport
Expense tracking			
Mileage		TaxMileage app	
Paperless statements		Evernote	
Contracts / agreements			

	More left brain / list oriented	More right brain / visual	Advanced business stages
Online Marketing			
Opt-in / e-list / autoresponder	MailChimp, AWebber Constant Contact iContact		InfusionSoft Ontraport
Shopping cart	1ShoppingCart Shopify WooCommerce	PayPal	InfusionSoft
Website / blog	WordPress		
Social media	LinkedIn	FB, Twitter, Instagram, Pinterest	HootSuite
Analytics / SEO			
Product download hosting			
JV / alliance	AWebber DealGuardian		InfusionSoft Ontraport

	More left brain / list oriented	More right brain / visual	Advanced business stages
Event Planning / Logistics			
Travel planning		TripIt	
Venue options	Excel		
Catering plan			
Handouts and gifts			
Relationship Management			
Prospecting	Insightly, IQTell vTiger, Agile	InfoFlo ReallySimple Hubspot	InfusionSoft ACT SalesForce
Speaking opportunities			
Client program status			
Team communication	Teamwork	Google, Evernote	Asana, Podio, Slack

The LifeHacker website also offers regular "best of" lists.

Choose Your Allies

Your downloaded gift package includes a worksheet you can use for this!

Personal Style

Your first consideration is whether the tool is right for YOU. If it doesn't feel right, you won't use it. End of story. As you look at the layout of tool interfaces and the flow of what they accomplish, keep in mind:

- Right brain (visual, spatial) / Left brain (list, text)
- Task focused / People focused
- Self only / Team access

Look at how you would **get daily information into the tool**, as well as how you would search and find it again, **and get it back out**!

How Well It Does What It Does

I recommend making yourself a checklist of what you want to have, then compare each tool against the checklist. Score each tool from 1 to 10 on each area and see which one comes out with the best overall score. Nothing off the shelf is likely to be a perfect match. You'll need to compromise and use your intuition (gut check) to know whether that's really the best match for you.

When I worked at Hewlett-Packard, we used a FURPS model to evaluate software. (Everything in the computer world has an acronym!) The letters stand for:

Functionality:

- Does the job (you get to define)

- Integration / synchronization across tools
- Multiple projects
- Cloud and offline access

Usability:

- "Pleasing" interface, visibility of what you need to see on one screen (and no distractions)
- Customizable / configurable
- Collaboration / sharing

Reliability:

- Upgrade paths
- Early adopter or established product
- Security
- Backups

Performance:

- Cost structure (number of users, amount of storage) (Price/performance point)
- Speed of access, search, download

Support:

- Device or OS availability
- Support contract or help website
- Online community or forum

You can add any specific areas to your comparison sheet as you discover them.

Integration Hub

For whatever tools you choose, collect a set that all integrate with the same hub. For example, I use a contact manager, task manager, and calendar that all coordinate with Google. I can put information into one tool, and it gets transferred to Google and subsequently shows up in the other tools. Note, though, that I don't actually use Google's tool interfaces!

Another common hub is Apple.

Business Stage

As your business grows, you can expect to outgrow your early-stage tools. That's fine. Starting out with tools that are too cumbersome slows you down and inflates your expenses.

- Stage 1: Getting first clients, figuring out messaging
- Stage 2: Consistent profit, one primary delivery
- Stage 3: Expand beyond one delivery, hire team
- Stage 4: Legacy, self-running

Avoid Lock-In

Your business will grow. Tool companies get acquired. They go new directions. Innovations appear in the marketplace.

Before you commit to a specific tool, determine what it takes to migrate your data back out of it so that you could move to a different provider. Exporting to comma separated variables (CSV) is often sufficient.

Also make sure the tool has a backup facility, or you can back up the data in case your system or their server crashes.

Do Your Homework to Find the Fit

I have to admit that I have no idea how people can buy new shoes online! You can't adequately evaluate any tool from what someone else says about it. You can use reviews to create a short list, but you'll only know for sure when you sign up, create an account, and start entering a slice of your information. Most have a free trial level or trial period.

You can expect to investigate a couple tools in each category. Go ahead and enter one project or set up one organization.

- How easy is it for YOU to enter information in the tool?
- Especially, how easy is it for YOU to see what's going on and find things again?
- Is the tool sharable with an assistant?
- And what does it cost to use?

Walk in it for a while to see if it's going to rub the wrong way and give you mental blisters. By investing some time here, **while staying focused on who YOU are**, you'll know you have a good fit and a tool set you can trust yourself to actually use.

Chapter 22
Designing to Use
Your Tools Elegantly

Don't you hate it when you know you put a piece of information in the "Current" folder, but when you go to look on your hard disk, the folders are "Prospects," "Clients," and "Signed Up"? Wait, was it in Evernote? No, the notebooks are "Past," "Present," and "Future." Oh, yeah! The "Current" folder is in your e-mail program!

Here's a gift you can give yourself: structure all your storage using the same set of names and organization. Consistency makes it easier for you to file things away and far quicker to find them again!

Breathe in. Breathe out.

What Are You Storing and Why?

We store things so that we can refer back to them, preferably in context. Most tools now have three ways to let us find things again:

- Hierarchical (folder) storage
- Tags or labels
- Search features

When we're building an integrated business lifestyle, we want to create the same quality of experience that brings us joy across our personal and professional endeavors. Consider these as **two wings of a bird that work together to uplift the center** (purpose), or perhaps two wings of a butterfly, with lovely designs and colorings within.

Let's design a structure that has a place for every kind of thing you do. Start with the roles you play, like wife, parent, business owner, friend, and so on. You probably wouldn't name a folder "Wife," but it can remind you to set up a place for things related to "Marriage."

You'll want to include placeholders for the things that motivate your actions—spiritual, health, travel, and learning. Also remember the fun stuff—hobbies, activities, shopping, and any other area for which you research and collect information.

When you get to your "Professional" wing, you can use the areas from the Circles of Success business plan.

Here are more ideas to spark your list:

Personal	Professional
• Relationships	•Career / occupation(s)
• Family	• Work 1
• Marriage / relationship	• Work 2
• Community / friends	• Volunteer / service / giving back
•Hobby / fun / recreation	•Operations
• Pet	• Money / finance
• Vehicles	• Receipts
• Creativity	• Statements
•Travel	• Taxes
•Spiritual / inspiration	• Shopping: wish lists, gift ideas
• Purpose / motivation	• Legal , licenses
• Humor / quotes	• Computer / software
•Health / well being / self-care	• Marketing
• Exercise	• Research and development
• Nutrition / recipes	• Lifelong learning / education
• Healing	• Personal growth
• Appearance	• Professional growth
•Home / housing / lifestyle	• Past classes
• Environment	• Interests
• Vehicles	• Being coached
	•Specific hot projects
	• Move
	• Launch
	• Current training

There is no one right answer for this, so **you can't get it wrong**. And as women, we know things continually evolve and change, so **you can't get it right forever**, either. Just start with your own list of categories for each wing, and maybe one level below that for each area. Some tools may have more levels; just keep them consistent where you use them.

Your free gift pack includes this butterfly image.
Put your purpose/mission in the center,
along with the qualities of experience you want in your life journey.

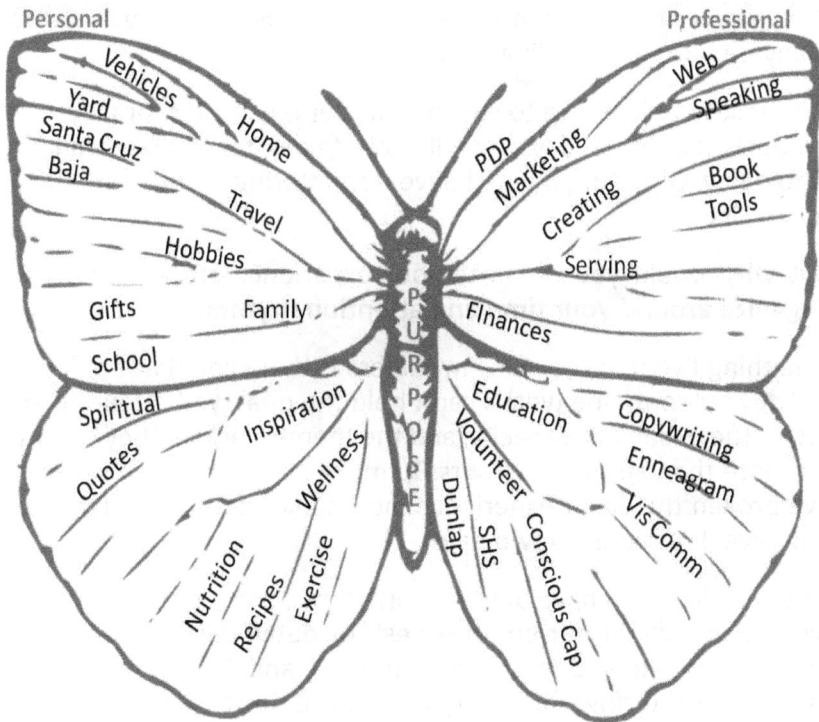

Note that travel can be both personal and professional. You can keep two locations for tax purposes, or you can choose to put it where you have more "room." Using your own structure consistently is the most important thing.

Now take the time to get the tools you're already using aligned to support you (you can set up the new ones as you go):

- Evernote notebooks and tags
- E-mail folders or labels
- Hard disk folders and cloud folders
- Action management projects
- Contact categories or organizations
- Quicken (finance) categories and tags or Quickbooks chart of accounts

You Don't Have to Eat the Elephant All at Once

Breaking your projects into activities or tasks seems obvious, but many people ask how "big" a task should be.

For most people, three to seven tasks per day makes for awesome productivity. Some days, you'll have fewer tasks that span the whole day. Other days, you'll have a smattering of different pieces to polish off.

But why would you organize your experience around the task? **Organize around your time and attention rhythm**.

One thing I've realized since my illness is that I could not pull off a VIP day for someone (yet). I can't hold the quality of attention and focus, the expansive capacity, and the theme tracking they deserve for more than about two hours. To make my work match my style, I've broken the client experience into intake sessions on two days and reveal sessions on two days.

Not only do we all have unique biorhythms, times of the day when we're generally at our creative best, or detail best, we also have attention-rhythms. Depending on the task and the time of day, we may get in the flow for ninety minutes. Or just twenty. Then we need a brief "change of scenery" to come back fresh and fired up. Otherwise, we start to fade and can easily fall prey to surfing or dawdling. Find your attention-rhythm for various times of the day and types of tasks. None of them are wrong—just knowing is your key!

Now here's how to design your route: For items where you have a longer attention-rhythm, plan for about ninety minutes of flow, a ten minute break, and ninety more minutes of flow. When you see one of those coming on your task horizon, gift yourself that full block of time without distractions or interruptions.

For things that come in shorter spurts of attention, go for twenty minutes on, five minutes off, three times in a row as described in the Pomodoro method.

Then you've done "enough for now." Let it go and move to something different with a clear conscience.

Chapter 23
Install, Configure, and Move In

Having chosen tools specifically to fit your style and business, actually starting to use them is... a hassle. Yeah, I know. Plus, it is also your **"business self-care" to set yourself up to succeed**, have more free time and attention, and enjoy the whole process more. Then you'll be able to delegate, too.

Select one tool at a time to make things easier for you. My suggestion would be to get your to-do list system fully supportive first. That's the one that helps you get through EVERYthing else.

After that, look for where you have the most mess or frustration. Generally, your personal tools come before the pillar tools, but not always. Look to your e-mail inbox and folders and get them self-managing. Consolidate if you have two (or more) sets of contacts. Consolidate multiple calendars if you have them.

Next come the tools that lead most directly to cash flow for the business model/strategy in your Big Picture. E-mail list and autoresponder can be a huge boon. Or it might be prospect tracking and follow-up. Or logistics and scheduling around delivering workshops or retreats. Again, don't be drawn in by the latest tool ad that floats through your Facebook feed. **Be intentional and On Purpose** about what's next to build out on your calendar.

Commit to Using the New

Your first step is often to "export" data from your old way (if it was on the computer) and "import" what you can into your new system. Beyond that, draw a line in the sand (of time) and commit to using your new system from here forward. No, you never have to go back and put "old" things into the system unless they are relevant to your actions and interactions today and tomorrow. If you force it into an overwhelming time sink to transfer all the historical data over, you'll never get around to starting.

If you ever need to do historical research, you'll just have to go through your old way (like you would have anyway) *and* your new way. But that's not today. Today you want to **focus on taking your purpose forward in the world**.

One of the biggest pieces of your commitment is to **use the system even when things get tight** over the next few weeks! Don't fall back to sticky notes just when you need the self-support!

Onboarding Yourself

Getting the system set up takes some time. **Plan it in**. Getting used to using it also takes time—not all in one sitting, but over a few days or weeks. Be patient and gentle with yourself. It'll be worth it!

It's a process: allow time to unpack and remember where things are.

Expect to rearrange the furniture—be adaptable.

Focus on learning to do one kind of task at a time that you can really use, rather than reading the manual from front to back. Document as you go and upgrade the notes as you discover tips and shortcuts.

Training and Community

You probably do not need to go through every training video or FAQ your new tool offers. On the other hand, the "getting started" sessions can be real time-savers in your orientation. Use all the resources at your disposal wisely.

Many tools have active forum communities on their website or on Facebook. Get plugged in and see what shortcuts the experts are tossing around.

Chapter 24
Configure Project and
Task Manager

This is one of the biggest needs I see among today's business-women—how to keep track of everything while giving attention to what matters most. So let's dive deeper into how you would set up whichever tool you chose for managing your to-do list.

First Create the Containers: Projects

Create a project for each of the areas on your butterfly wings. If your chosen tool allows a hierarchy of folders, great! If it is more "flat," you can simulate a hierarchy by using what would have been a folder name as a prefix before the project or area.

For example, under Hobbies, I might want Knitting, Painting, Beading, Gardening. If I could not have a Hobbies "folder," I would use the names Hobby:Knit, Hobby:Paint, Hobby:Bead, Hobby:Garden. That way, they'd all be grouped together when I looked at a list.

Within your business, I recommend using the Circles of Success areas. You'll probably want a separate container for each of your clients. You may need to break out your marketing efforts further.

Speaking to hold prospective speaking opportunities, track your conversations, and develop your talks

- Online marketing to capture everything from developing your opt-in gift and planning e-mail campaigns, to selecting and running your e-commerce and monitoring your analytics
- Networking to help you plan for groups to attend, set your objective for each, and keep track of whom you meet
- Group program launch (or any launch) so that you can develop the program as well as identify potential affiliate partners and when blog posts and e-mails go out
- Book development to have an e-book that supports your business, identify voice, determine objectives, design flow, and track your progress to get it written and edited

Next Prepare Your Groups for Time and Energy

For some tools, you'll set these up as tags. For others, they are database fields. Either way, the key is that you can apply these across ALL your project containers.

Note: These tags are created for you when you set up the Evernote business planning notebooks on your free gift!

Configure Meaningful Priorities

1—This Week

2—Next Week

3—Next Month

4—Later

5—Someday

6—Waiting

By putting the numbers in front of these, they'll sort in the order you should work on them.

Configure Energy Context

Traditional time management systems use "context" to mean where you're sitting. Group all your computer-related tasks. Group all your phone-related tasks. But some phone calls are mundane, and some require you to have all your wits about you! (And practically *every*thing happens at the computer.)

This is one of the key features of Purposetivity. We collect tasks together by the quality of engagement or the kind of energy they require! Then when you're in a creative mood, you can see at a glance which activities are aligned and most on purpose. Or when you're whipped at the end of the day, you can see if there's one more mindless thing you can have off the plate before tomorrow.

The energy levels I use are:

> **Active**: Physical. Cleaning, moving, exercise, yard
>
> **Calm**: Quiet. Contemplation, difficult conversations, catching up on audios
>
> **Clarity**: Mental (left brain). Details, precision, education
>
> **Connecting**: Heart. Welcoming, receptive
>
> **Creative**: All of me. Writing, inventing, designing
>
> **Mindless**: None. Insurance calls, making appointment

Invent or adapt as it suits YOU!

Dump in Everything You Can Find

OK, your next step is to do a **full brain dump** into the tasks, as well as every scrap of paper and napkin you have actionable tasks written on.

Go through each project area and see if any other activities come to the surface. Is it complete?

Look around your office and note what you've been meaning to get done.

Walk around your house with a notepad. Consider each member of your family and close friends. What have you been meaning to take care of?

What are the repeated tasks you do every week? Every month? By season (for example, winterizing)? Add those in and use the tool's repeat function if it has one.

Ideas that are not actionable can go in Evernote. These would be things like "wish list" or "gift ideas."

You may be able to export from tools you currently use and import to your new tool, especially if you are moving from desktop to cloud. This really helps when you have separate lists on your computer and in an app on your phone.

As you do this, make sure at least the **immediate things are marked as priority 1**.

In the future, prioritize and categorize as you go. You'll thank yourself!

Weekly Review: Don't Create with Your Mind Full

Just because all your tasks are now in the computer doesn't mean they're getting done! Those scraps of paper on your desk (and everywhere else) reminded you to do stuff when you saw them. To make your automated process work, YOU have to go look at your to-do list.

Set yourself a personal promise (and a recurring task) to review your complete set of Actions once each week. You may choose the end of the week (Sunday evening) or the start of the week (Monday morning) in preparation for the coming week.

Your first step is to make sure it is, in fact, your complete set. Dump everything you can think of into your overall list from wherever you've collected action items (your head, your purse, that napkin, ...).

Now review everything you had marked "This Week." Done? Check it off! Not really going to happen? Be honest and move it to "Next Week." Ideally only the things you're really, honestly going to DO this week should be in this list. The rest is noise for now, and that doesn't help your sanity. If you finish everything, you can always recheck and pull in the next batch. If you've taken your step and now it's in someone else's lap, move it to "Waiting" and add that contact info, along with when you should check back with them.

The third step is to review the "Next Week" list and adjust any tasks that need to be pulled in or pushed out. You'll also want to check the later categories to see if anything is coming up on your horizon.

Two-Minute Warning: Distraction to DONE

For kids, we had the two-second rule: If it fell on the floor and was there for under two seconds, it was still safe to pick up and eat. (They survived.)

For sanity, we have the two-minute rule: if it falls on your plate (e-mail, phone, paper) and would take under two minutes to complete, do it now!

It's just not worth the time to create a task to come back to it. And if you stash it somewhere (sticky notes, anyone?), you're just going to end up with a "junk drawer" mishmash. Then when you get around to tackling that awful pile, you'll have a different context to look up for every item. Just do it while you have it in front of you and call it DONE.

And if you DO end up with The Pile, play the game seen on children's TV shows called "Two Minute Cleanup." Set a timer (or not) for two minutes and polish off or put away as many things as you can. Then stop.

Piles and clutter and unfinished business lurking in the corners of our space are distracting and draining.

Batching It

Not everything needs to be handled the instant it arrives. This is the paradox of the "Two-Minute Warning."

Turn off e-mail notifications and check and handle e-mails only three or four specific times per day. Do the same for social media notifications and text messaging.

Whenever you have the option, schedule your bill payments to happen on the same day of the month as each other so that you only attend to monthly things all at once. For others, collect them during the week and have a "bookkeeping" time when you pay and balance them once for the week.

Plan these activities around your biorhythm—don't do follow-up during your most creative hours! And don't try to manage finances during your connecting zone! It's YOURS to match up with your preferences, so grab it.

Spurts

The human brain has rhythms. We are not precisely consistent machines. Rather than beating yourself to get something done, work WITH your rhythm. Work for a bit, then take a break and come back. The break needs to truly get you away from the task, but only briefly (or you'll get sucked into something else!).

The Pomodoro technique describes it like this: set a timer for 20 or 25 minutes. This is about how long most people can truly hold focus. Tell yourself, "I can do ANYthing for just 20 minutes." And dive into the deep end!

When the timer goes off, take a five-minute break. Move, change pace. Nourish your body. Hug your dog.

Come BACK! After the five-minute break, come back and set your timer for another 20 minutes.

After three rounds, you can go on to a different task. You've probably spent the quality energy for this one for now.

Fuel to Want to Use Tools

Setting up new habits generally feels awkward at first. Especially when things get intense, our tendency is to bag the new and return to the old way. When you find yourself drifting in this direction, take a moment to **review the "Why" in your business plan**. Remember that **old patterns can't support new growth**. Take a deep breath and use the crisis to propel you to better and better alignment and familiarity with tools that fit your future.

Joining tool user communities can be hugely beneficial. Not only can you often get quick answers to glitches in your use, you will be inspired by how others are building their systems. You can create a Pinterest board if you want, for innovations you want to check out.

Chapter 25
Review Your Business Model and Implementation Plan

Things change. Life changes. The market changes. Technology changes. We change.

Luckily, you've built that in!

The days of the five-year business plan are pretty much over (unless you are seeking financing). Being doggedly committed to a plan, just 'cause you said you would, is a recipe destined to fall in the middle like a soufflé. **The new game is to remain aligned** with your lifestyle choices, your values, and your clients' needs **while all of it is in motion,** like a dance. It's about relationship, not blinders.

Now, you can't be reconsidering every day. That kind of second guessing and waffling is exhausting and leads to a lot of SBO purchases. If you leave it all until New Year's, you'll miss a lot of indicators and opportunities.

Quarterly tends to be a good balance.

Whether you use fiscal quarters and check in at the start of January, April, July, and October, or use the wheel of the year and review on solstices and equinoxes, taking time to look at what's working and what's not serving is a crucial part of the Purposetivity way.

What Happens in a Quarterly Review?

Look at each area in your life and business plan. Note any "external" changes that are obviously visible. Also look at each of your directional statements and values in that area to see if any start to feel scratchy, like outgrown clothes from the inside. The outcome of the review is a list of what to do more of and what to do less of.

Watch for things to add in AND things that are falling away. What is feeling complete for this season? What needs to come on board for next season?

As you go along, you'll generate many (many!) possibilities. Capture them in your task management tool and prioritize them at the end of your session.

Start with Your Mission Statement

Whatever it looks like to you, review your mission and vision before looking over your activities and results. That's where Purposetivity begins!

Review Each Area of Lifestyle: Family Situation, Wellness, etc.

Have your kids changed their school situation (off for the summer or back to school)? Seasonal sports or extra-curricular activities? How do you *want* that to affect your focus on work?

Has anything changed with other family members?

How is your health? Is your body asking for more nutrients? A break from stressors? Movement? Retreat?

How is the household running? Are there seasonal tasks that need to be factored in? (Add them to your task management tool.)

Check in with your spiritual self. Is anything being called for?

Are there new activities or shifts in your community or social groups?

Review your life meters to see if new improvements are ready to come on board.

Review Each Area of Circles of Success from Your Business Plan

This is primarily looking from the perspective inside your business. It's both a healthy, honest critique and a heartfelt, creative brainstorm.

Inspired Vision

Are things unfolding in alignment with your vision?

Are you walking your talk?

Is there more you want to articulate clearly (about who you are, what you offer, how the world changes, how people are to be treated, etc.)?

Succulent Indicators

Print a new pyramid and fill in your gut feeling for how you're doing qualitatively.

How many people are you touching? How often? At what depth?

Recognize which of your activities is actually generating the results you want, both in terms of revenue and fulfillment. Review analytics to see which activities align with revenue (or not).

Identify which activities are not producing for you. Do they require more time to grow, or are they simply not a fit for you or your clients?

Notice where your largest areas of expense are—both financial and in your personal energy. Are they aligned with your values? Are there areas where increasing your investment would increase your results even more?

What trends are you spotting?

Joyful Communication

Review the communication model(s) you have in place. Which are producing responses and interaction? Which are nonproductive?

Consider your implementation plan for what you thought would be the next step. Is it still the right next step? Is it time to proceed or still time to integrate the last bite?

Review the recent tone of your communications to ensure it aligns with your vision of service in the world. It can be all too easy to slip into arguing against what we don't want rather than continuing to take a stand for what we do want.

Who are you talking to? Are there new areas or groups you're inspired to reach out to?

How are you connecting? How often are you connecting?

What are you saying? What do you want to be saying?

What might be the bottom 10% that you'd release?

Exuberant Creativity

How healthy is each of your products or programs? Do any of them need tweaking?

What is bubbling up from your soul to be shared next with the people you serve? What are they calling forth from you?

How well are you making time and space to actually create?

Celebrating Delivery

How are sessions going? How would you gauge your clients' level of delight?

How are group programs flowing? Are you seeing all the forms of results (outcomes, connections, testimonials, etc.) that you want?

How many ways are you providing value, and in what forms?

Is there a low producer that needs to be dropped or revamped?

Is there something seasonal on the horizon?

Supportive Systems

Which processes and tools feel supportive and right on?

Which feel like leaky buckets?

Which are you outgrowing (that is, they were working fine, but with your new expansions, they don't have what you need anymore)?

What new processes need to be defined for the growth you're anticipating?

Inner Adventures

How are you keeping up with developments in your field? Techniques in your craft?

What areas of business ownership are ready to be addressed?

How are you feeding your mind, your heart, your body, and your soul through your body?

What is complete and ready to be left behind?

What do you crave more of?

Ask Clients and Tribe What's Working or Not

This is a great time to provide a survey to your people to find out where their interests are shifting, what they're growing into, and what they'd really like to have from you.

You can informally check in with clients as you see them, or create a simple list of questions through Survey Monkey (free). Letting people know what you heard can start a great discussion!

New Opportunities on the Horizon

Now take it from outside your business and look in. What trends have you noticed "out there" in the market that may be relevant to bring in? Have you been invited to speak or to co-create an offering?

What new market areas are emerging?

What playgrounds have you been invited to play in? Do you have new partners or playmates?

What educational opportunities are opening up?

Where can you mentor or be mentored?

Remember, you'll always come up with far more opportunities than could possibly fit into the next quarter! You can't do everything first—and you don't need to. Use your intuitive tools (feel into your body) to choose what falls off your plate and what comes on your plate that leads to the most growth and delight and fulfillment for you!

Update Your Plans

With all these new ideas and opportunities, you need to prioritize which ones fit first in your overall plan. For the new ideas coming into your game, list the tasks to get them going. The rest can be categorized as "Later" in your task management system.

Section 3
Expand and Evolve

Chapter 26
The Transformational Workplace: Replace Rules with Values

Value Your Values

Whereas your style has to do with how you want to experience yourself and your interaction with your environment, values are slanted more toward how we prefer to interact with other people, what our expectations are, and what makes us feel respected, appreciated, etc.

1. In the following partial list, circle all values that resonate with you. You will find a complete list in the worksheets you downloaded previously.

Abundance	Accountability	Accuracy	Achievement	Adventure
Ambition	Assertiveness	Balance	Beauty	Belonging
Brilliance	Calm	Challenge	Certainty	Clarity
Collaboration	Commitment	Communication	Compassion	Competence
Competition	Confidence	Connection	Consciousness	Consistency
Contribution	Control	Courage	Creativity	Curiosity
Decisiveness	Democracy	Dependability	Devotion	Discipline
Diversity	Effectiveness	Efficiency	Encouragement	Enthusiasm
Equality	Excellence	Fairness	Fame	Family
Flexibility	Focus	Freedom	Fun	Generosity
Gratitude	Growth	Harmony	Helpfulness	Honesty
Humility	Humor	Independence	Innovation	Inspiration
Integrity	Joy	Kindness	Leadership	Love
Loyalty	Meaning	Openness	Organization	Passion
Peace	Positivity	Practicality	Proactivity	Professionalism
Presence	Quality	Recognition	Resourcefulness	Respect
Simplicity	Speed	Teamwork	Truth	Unity
Variety	Vision	Well-being	Wisdom	

2. Of all the possibly important values, write down your top ten in any order:

2.1.

2.2.

2.3.

2.4.

2.5.

2.6.

2.7.

2.8.

2.9.

3. Pair up the values and determine "If I could satisfy only one of these, which would matter most to me?" Continue to thin the list until you determine your top three values.

    3.1.

    3.2.

    3.3.

4. For each of your top three, how can you tell (what do you see, hear, sense) when someone expresses it and when someone doesn't?

5. For each of your top three, how does it show up when you express it? How does it sometimes come out sideways (negative expression)?

6. Are there any of your values that could cause internal conflicts within your own psyche (perhaps control and creativity, for example)?

Chapter 27
Hire for Values
Before Capabilities

Many, many people have competency in web page management or follow-up calls. Out of all those people, you want to hire the one(s) who resonate with your values—for both interactions with you and to represent you to the world.

When you bring someone onto your team and "they don't work out," often the reason can be traced back to mismatched values. There is no reason you should have to "put up with" a team member who makes you uncomfortable, creates conflict, or causes unmet expectations—so long as you make things clear and open up front.

What Do You Want?

Of course your job description needs to include the tasks you want performed and the level of "ownership" you expect.

Also recognize which skill sets you expect someone to have already developed in the pay range you're offering, and what training you will be providing. In addition to skill set, be specific about what hardware and software tools you provide and which ones you expect them to have licensed. In this time of diverse tech cultures, be clear about how professional or casual you want communication to be (for example, are common texting abbreviations going to be acceptable in customer communications?).

As you're starting to build your company culture, consider the following:

- To what degree do you value diversity? How important is language or accent to you?

- To what degree do you prefer globalization or "shop local" and keeping jobs in your country? How much does time zone availability matter to you?

- Will your hiring match your marketing? For example, are you looking to charge premium prices but undercut rates paid to your providers?

- Which legal guidelines for discrimination based on age, religion, gender, race, etc. do you need to consider for your location? While you may have more flexibility in contract hiring than employees, still be cognizant of the boundaries.

Just as you've identified your own personal style, be clear about whether you're hiring matching or complementary skills. If you are a "people person," are you looking for someone who is also a people person? Or do you want to complement that with someone who focuses more on tasks?

Taking it a layer deeper, write the qualitative aspects and expectations of how you want it to feel to work with your team members (and they with each other). How do you want things to feel when deadlines loom? When you write about this, include communication tones for letting people know dependencies, or what to do when exceptions come up or plans need to change. As much as possible, write clear examples of how matching values actually show up in your ideal team interactions and relationships.

Happy Business Owner Seeks Compatible Team Member

Now you're ready for the fun part! Write a playful "dating ad" that would appeal to values first and tasks second. Make it as clear and juicy as you can, as if you were going to be establishing a long-term partnership with this person (which you are). Put it out there!

Once you've gotten the wild one out of your system, you may want to tone it down (or not!) to write your request for assistance. Keep the qualitative, values-based statements first.

You can post your request to public forums, to your newsletter or blog, and ask strategic alliance partners whom they may know.

Determine hiring locations that are a probable match for your values. It may include open sites like Upwork.com, specific VA service sites like SuccessTroops.com, or someone you've met in a compatible local network meeting.

Select among Candidates

If you have only a few responses, you may be able to interview all of them. However, if you have an overload of candidates, you'll need to screen them and pick only the top handful to interview. Here you're just looking for any reason to set aside the majority of responses.

Remember the adage "How you do anything is how you do everything." You're going to be counting on this person.

- Is the response complete? If parts are missing now, you'll get partial work later.
- Is it coherent? Does it have a flow you can follow?
- Is it clear? Spelling errors or sloppy communication layout will be unacceptable in some positions.
- Is it concise? Does it match the level of personalization and directness that you want to work with?
- Is it correct? For the top ten or twelve, go ahead to their listed references to verify their accuracy as best you can.

OK, now for the pile of No's, get centered and make an intuitive pass. Is there something about any one of these that still calls your attention? If the potential feels strong enough, add them back to the group to be interviewed.

Schedule Interviews

As you connect with each candidate, monitor how they treat the interaction. If you e-mail or leave a voice mail, do they respond promptly? Are they courteous and respectful (does their culture appear to be a match)? How flexible is their scheduling?

Prepare Interview Questions

The best predictor of future behavior is past behavior. So develop a set of questions that help you hone in on how their values have shown up in their work. Look back to your description of how you want values to show up (and what constitutes a red flag or a lack of respect for a value for you). Your hires won't have the *same* values as you. You're hiring them because they fill a need you want to offload! But the relationship must be compatible.

Prepare some lead-in questions and make yourself an interview template. You can phrase questions like, "Give me an example of a time when you:"

- Chose _____ over what was common or easy
- Had to trade off between two things you value highly
- Could not meet a deadline or expectation
- Had a client who didn't give you what you needed on time
- Looked beyond the assignment and added value to the organization

What work are you really proud of?

What is most important to you in living a good life? How does that play out in your work?

When you use the same starter questions for everyone, you begin from a base of fairness.

If possible (and part of the job), set up a screen share and have them show you some of their work and style.

During the Interview

Relax and have fun—the way you would want everyday interactions to go. By letting your candidate feel at ease, you get to feel more of their natural authenticity so you know better whether it will be a match to work together.

Recording the conversation is generally not necessary, but be sure to take notes. By the time you've chatted with three or twelve people, remembering who said what gets a little fuzzy. Telling the candidate to pause a moment so that you can take notes is perfectly fine.

Attend to nonverbal cues and pauses. Notice when and how long a candidate hesitates before continuing. It may be they're just trying to remember an example, yet bringing it to your consciousness can be helpful.

Take some questions deeper if you feel called. For example, you can ask, "How did that make you feel?" Establishing rapport is important, yet don't fill the time with stories to match theirs. Let them tell more about their experience and where they took it.

Expect a savvy VA to also be interviewing you! They don't want to add a deadbeat or difficult client to their day either.

Responding to Candidates (Yes or No)

Each candidate you talk with deserves a response.

First, contact the person you most want to work with and see if they felt it was a match. Verify that your scheduling and finances mesh well.

Once you have determined whom you do want to hire, respond to each of the other candidates to let them know it is not a match at this time. If you are feeling generous, the greatest gift you can give them is feedback. Where did they come across really well? What seemed to be a mismatch? Did anything really seem off about the interaction? A real friend will tell you when you have spinach in your teeth.

Chapter 28
You Are a Transformational Messenger. Are You a Transformational Boss?

What you really want is to develop people who can own "departments" of your business and just take them over and get it right. More than someone to follow rules you write to today's marketplace, you want them to recognize the quality of play you're in and continuously adapt those *values* forward as the world evolves. You are here (in business) to create leaders, to empower people. Start with whom you hire.

You are no longer operating as an island. You need to expand your awareness to include activities that are not through your hands. No, you don't need to track and micro-manage every step. But you are part of a dance now, and they can only follow if you lead.

In essence, the "Inner Adventures" Circle of Success (human resources) now becomes "Leadership Adventures" for self and others. You must continue to sharpen your own saw AND expand your awareness to empower and grow team members.

The way you treat your team determines how they treat your audience. Walk your talk!

Compliance with Values Becomes Your Team Culture

As you bring someone on board, have a meeting to go over tasks and procedures. Also have a meeting to go over values and cultural expectations—in both directions!

What do you need to do to help them be successful in supporting you?

Use your notes from how you expect your values to show up, when you feel respected or appreciated or not.

Find out the same from your team. Take notes if you need to. Consider that a top VA will be "firing" their bottom 10% of clients every year. When you find a good one, you'd better let them know in language they understand.

By having this discussion on values and interaction styles. For example, "Do you prefer e-mail, text, or voice?" You maximize the flowing nature of your work environment. Rigid rules like "every e-mail must be answered within sixty minutes" may lead to compliance, but never to empowerment. Even though so many of the "classic" management books will tell you to set up hierarchy and rules, if you're here, that's no longer an appropriate approach to our world (if it ever was).

Things you should discuss include: hours of availability, turnaround time, best method of contact, language, and tone. And LISTEN to their expectations. If this person expects spontaneous time off for kid activities, consider whether that is part of your culture (wholistic lifestyle), or if you'd be better off with a child-free hire.

How to Notice, Reward, Adjust Behavior

It's up to you to stay present and attuned enough to your own experience to notice when your values are being met or missed.

Review your list of how you know and keep it handy when you're in meetings with your assistant(s).

Ideally at the closure of each meeting, but at least on a monthly review basis, let your assistant know how you're FEELING when working with them. And let them know the specific behaviors (or lack thereof) that are contributing to your experience. Feedback with the intent to improve the relationship shows important trust and respect.

When you and your assistant are not on the same wavelength, especially on items that were not in the original description but are now feeling scratchy, call a team time-out and address it. Let the person know what is uncomfortable, what impact that has on you or the objectives, and what you would like to see instead.

You might want to consider the "Search Inside Yourself" emotional intelligence leadership program that originated at Google.

Basis for Empowerment

When team members truly embody the business values and fully understand the business objectives, you have empowered them to "own" their piece of the business. **The more you create empowered team members, the more freedom you have to put your attention on what matters most to you**.

Really turning over control of a process or a whole "department" in one of your Circles of Success requires significant trust. Trust that the job will get done. Trust that it will be done in a way that is aligned with you and your values. Trust that it will integrate with other people's pieces.

Chapter 29
Delegate Effectively

Document Your Design

Hopefully you've been "documenting everything you touch" as recommended previously and you have a nice collection of procedures. If not, now's the time.

Either way, everything you can do to communicate clearly and to prepare everyone on the team makes things run smoother. The most important part is **defining the interfaces to lead to clear expectations and harmony**.

1. Sketch out (use sticky notes) the larger flow you're working within, for example, the parts of a marketing launch if you want autoresponders entered.

2. Identify whose job each step is.

3. Draw communication arrows from one step to the next. Number the arrows.

4. For each arrow IN end, what information needs to flow along it for the next person to be successful? What needs to be in place in the background? What already needs to be done?

5. For each arrow OUT end, what are the specific deliverables (content, format, location) when that step is complete?

6. Go back to each sticky note (step) and write a "recipe" for what needs to happen with the information coming in, to transform it to the results going out. The more detail you can include the better, especially if it's a task you've been doing yourself. Numbered steps with screenshots will minimize the number of "I'm confused" calls later.

You may choose to document these in a shared Evernote notebook or as documents on a shared drive. Just be sure your team knows where to find them!

If you would like more detailed steps for this section, check out my online course, "VA Ready in 60 Days or Less."

Onboarding Team Members

One of the most frequent laments I've heard is a business owner who has gone ahead and hired someone to handle some area for them (like social media), then not gotten the results they expected and had difficult conflicts in style to try to "get their money's worth."

Especially when you are hiring across generations or other cultural diversity, you need clarity.

As we already discussed, you need to set cultural expectations. Following that, you'll need to ensure the VA is prepared for success with each actual task you're delegating. Provide written information and do a walk-through (different learning types). You're *intentionally* hiring someone who is not like you! Ask for questions.

Define mutual success together: for your business to grow and for both of you to enjoy it. This is where your Conscious Capitalism leadership and culture muscles get built. What do they need to train you to do or not do? (Waiting for copy from a manager who never gets around to it makes me feel unimportant and like it doesn't matter when I DO get it.)

If you think you're hiring someone to do crisis management because *you* leave things until they are emergencies, you'd better be clear on that expectation up front. You may need to pay "emergency mode" rates or put them on retainer so that they don't need to balance your work with other clients'.

It's up to you to **keep them successful in making you successful**! Leadership is a special form of commitment.

Management by Objectives

If you need to micro-manage, you may as well do it yourself. But how do you pry your clenched fingers off the steering wheel?

Back in the heyday, a key part of Hewlett-Packard was Management by Objectives. MBOs (because after all, as a computer company we had to have acronyms!) ensured that team members were contributing to a common goal without impinging their creative genius or micro-managing their "how." Using MBOs (which might also be Monthly Business Objectives) with your team also helps keep you out of the gray area where a contractor becomes an employee (with payroll taxes due) because you control when, where, and how they do their tasks.

A mantra that can help you let go is "Excellence is better than perfection." "Done" is also much better than stuck or spinning feeling overwhelmed where you cannot possibly get it all done yourself!

Know Your Desired Outcome and What It Contributes to (and what that contributes to)

Of all the processes in your business, select the (next) one you want off your plate. It might be follow-up calls or autoresponder setup or bookkeeping.

Now, what is the outcome when that process goes well?

How does it contribute to the big picture of your business and lifestyle success?

Know How You'll Know

Recognize the difference between measuring outcomes and counting tasks. The purpose of follow-up calls is to engage people on your calendar for strategy sessions. The number of calls per day, or per hour, is very secondary if they aren't effective calls!

You can also set achievement levels, such as two, ten, or twenty sessions scheduled.

One of the quick ways to get clear on how to know when it's done well is to brainstorm what you *don't* want. It's a stepping stone to documenting what you do want. Then throw away the "no, thank you" list!

Include qualitative feedback like having prospects comment on how respectful or fun (based on your business's values) the interaction was.

Know the Process and Tools to Approach It

Once you have identified the process you want to be supported, you know which tool set is involved. Social media campaigns involve log-ins and use of social media tools (Facebook, LinkedIn, Twitter, Instagram, etc.). E-mail campaigns require autoresponder expertise with MailChimp, AWebber, InfusionSoft, etc. These are very different levels of technical complexity you'll be hiring for!

Get (or Train) the Right Person for the Job

If this is not an assignment to a VA already on your team, see the previous chapter for "Hire for values before capabilities."

If you choose to hire someone who does not already have expertise with the particular tools your business uses, build in time to patiently train your candidate up to speed.

Assign SMART Objectives

As you're setting out the objectives for your VA, use the same guidelines as when you set goals for yourself! Make sure they include the qualities that are SMART.

Specific – Be precise in what you want to have done and the manner or approach (using values) to embarking on it.

Measurable – Clarify how you will measure outcomes, both quantitatively and qualitatively. If you are also including tasks toward outcomes (like number of social posts toward an engagement objective), document that as well.

Achievable – You must get input from your contractor to ensure what you have in mind is possible. If it's a task you've handled yourself in the past, you know what it takes for *you* to do it. Keep in mind that someone else may not work at the same speed as you (could be slower OR faster!). If it's a new area coming into your business, find out a reasonable completion rate from the person performing the job. Over time, you'll learn how accurate they are with their estimates, and you can adjust accordingly. I had some engineers on my team whose estimates I consistently doubled in my planning; others generally included 10% too much time!

Relevant – Include the context and outcome of the outcome for your person. You want them enrolled as an active team member, not just a cog in your wheel.

Timely – When does the overall objective need to be complete? And what are the key milestones to ensure you're all on track along the way?

Once you've been working with your VA for some time, you may co-create these objectives more than delegate them.

Your gift packet includes a worksheet for monthly MBO with these columns.

Gain Agreement

When you discuss this plan with your assistant, make sure you have a shared understanding of the process as well as the results. Have them describe it back to you and welcome any questions to fill in missing details. You can't expect someone to succeed if they don't really understand.

Document expectations in both directions. Make sure you provide them with the process documents and tool access.

Also discuss the timeline and dependencies. **Expectations go both ways!** You need to provide them with what they need (usually copy) to be successful, and do it on time.

Monitor Status

You don't want to be a "dump and run" manager. Have your VA stay in touch on a regular basis that makes sense for the scope of the engagement: daily, weekly, or monthly updates or check-ins.

Let them know they're *encouraged* to let you know about potential difficulties early! It's not a mark of failure, and there's no "should" around figuring it all out by themselves. Honesty lets the whole team handle issues proactively to ensure the success of the big picture.

Typical things to include in an update:

- Progress toward next milestone
- Next step(s) on the horizon
- Check for roadblocks
- Suggested contingency plans
- Hours worked or budget used to date

Acknowledging, Celebrating, Gratitude, Appreciation

For goodness sakes don't get so driven on to the next project that you forget to celebrate milestones and completions! Celebration makes the effort worthwhile and **human appreciation can mean everything** to someone working as a VA from home.

Certainly verify completion of the objective. Then acknowledge your team members with:

- **Who**: Who you recognize as having contributed and to whose experience. It could include you, to another team member, and to clients or prospects.

- **What**: What did you see them do or say? What steps do you know they took along the way? In what ways did they have to rise to a challenge and grow? What have you achieved together?

- **Where**: While probably not geographical, think about where you really saw them show up, where they took initiative, where they went beyond the bare job description to ensure success, and where they were simply reliable— which counts for so much in building trusting relationships.

- **When**: When did they make themselves available or schedule flexibly? When did they recover from a goof, theirs or yours? When did they do whatever it took to get the job done?

- **How**: How did they show up? Recognize where values were honored and embodied. How was their attitude? Many qualitative aspects come into play in this space.

- **Why**: Reinforce why what they did matters, the ways in which it contributes to the mission and vision of the business. Why does it make a difference in your life to have them there? Why does it matter to clients? To the world?

Pay on time! Pay in all forms, including testimonials and referrals as well as finances. This is part of creating multiple forms of value for your stakeholders.

When you complete a large project or launch, schedule a separate debrief. Take time to review how things worked or could be better: assignment, process, communication, clarity, effectiveness, efficiency. Document improvements.

Closure and Termination

Even with the best of hiring practices and clearest of cultural and job expectations, sometimes people simply don't match. Other times, behaviors are clearly not in alignment with the culture. Showing up to call prospects while "under the influence" would be a good example. Extensive absenteeism, negativity or bullying behavior, inability to learn the skills ... sometimes it just doesn't work out.

When it's not a match, the person can hold your mission back. And frankly, you're probably holding them back when they need to be someplace else in their life.

As the motto goes, "Hire slowly, fire quickly."

Document specifically what the cause is. If it is something you have given feedback on, keep a record of those discussions.

Give the person as much notice as is safe. You want to be a good partner in letting them go find another position, but you don't want to expose your data and online presence to any malicious activity. When they are officially gone, be sure to change your passwords and access credentials and remove them from shared folders.

Chapter 30
Communication Style

Communication keeps things moving smoothly. Some communication is "hotter" than others. Status updates might just require a short e-mail when everything's on track. A major win calls for a celebration call or dinner!

We have so many tools and forms of communication these days. With smart phones, people have insidious expectations of being always available. Consider each channel of communication and how you prefer to interact. You can assign types of content and different channels "urgency factors" and write down how soon you expect to respond on each channel.

Possible communication channels:

- E-mail
- Text
- Phone call
- Social media message
- Team management tool chat or comment
- Zoom, Hangout, or Skype meeting

Based on timeliness and integration with other things you're working on—and your personal style!—how do you want to be informed or discuss:

- Assignments
- Status updates
- Potential risks recognized—possible problem on the horizon
- Exception reports—something went wrong
- Add-ons and redirects—when you want something changed
- Missed dependencies
- Completion

Include these communication guidelines in your procedures manual. You can set up special notifications so that you recognize urgent messages from your team. Encourage your team to put the action required in the subject for any e-mail! You could design a chart to show how quickly you agree to respond to types of messages on the various channels:

	E-mail	Text	Phone call	Social media message	Team management tool chat or comment	Zoom, Hangout, or Skype meeting
Assignments	24 hours	12 hours	4 hours unless teaching	12 hours	24 hours	
Status updates	24 hours				24 hours	
Potential risks recognized possible problem on the horizon	4 hours	2 hours	2 hours	2 hours	Don't use	
Exception reports— something went wrong	4 hours	2 hours	2 hours	2 hours	Don't use	
Add-ons and redirects— when you want something changed	24 hours	12 hours	8 hours	12 hours		
Missed dependencies	4 hours	2 hours	2 hours	2 hours	Document only	
Completion	4 hours	2 hours	2 hours	2 hours		

Select Team Automation Tools

When you bring team members into your picture and need to coordinate work, a new category of tool comes into your picture.

The primary tools you'll use in delegating to your VA involve communication, tasks, storage, and status. There's no point investing in a tool you'll never use because it just doesn't suit you. Refresh your personal style and preferences as you select tools at the team level, just as you did for personal productivity.

Choosing a team tool, or set of tools, includes all the considerations you looked at before. Sometimes you'll look at an integrated tool that provides all the features in one place. Other times you'll want point-tactic tools.

Some tools assume you and your team are actively engaged in developing an idea together and you want to have near-real-time engagement with everyone's ideas. For example, if you're a team doing branding and development on a website for a large customer launch, you might want graphics and copy and usability all working together collaboratively. These tools generally expect users to have them open and on the desktop at all times.

However, if you're a service professional (coach, therapist, healer) and you want your web team to go off and do things, notifying you only if they have questions, you don't want to have that open as well as e-mail. You may never even look into their collaboration tools.

When you're comparing tools, set up your objectives, then compare the tools against your desires rather than each other. In team tools, you'll want to consider how much gets shared and whether some areas can be kept private. Look at how tasks get assigned and status updates are communicated back to the team. Does the tool provide multiple types of visualization, from scheduling charts to card-sorting views? You may have to dig, but it's worth figuring out how much you'll be able to automate and repeat processes using templates. Will each team member be able to synchronize with their personal productivity tools (calendar, tasks) or have to track yet-another-interface? And as always, be sure to include an evaluation of security and backups.

- Collaboration tools to consider: Asana, Basecamp, Teamwork, Podio, Wrike
- Communication: Slack, Memeit
- Scheduling: Podio, Target Process, Easy Projects, Instagantt for Asana

In general, open source tools will be usable to you only if you have a full-time technical staff.

Clarity and Availability of Documentation

Choose how you make documentation available to your VA in the areas of:

- Processes, scripts, templates
- Access credentials
- Delivering copy or other content
- Calendar and CRM systems
- Client records
- Current assignment objectives and agreements

You might use a shared folder such as Google Drive or DropBox. You could use shared Evernote notebooks. Consider team management tools such as Asana, even if you minimize using them as a communication path. Least effective is simply e-mailing documents back and forth, hoping each person keeps track of the latest revision.

Please do NOT put log-ins and passwords into unsecured tools to share. Good password management tools like LastPass or Dashlane allow you to share them securely.

Chapter 31
Empowering Collaboration

The purpose aligned with your soul's intention and your heart's desire often requires more than your individual participation to see it through to fruition. **You belong to the purpose more than it belonging to you.** And as a member in the larger ecosystem, you have many forms of collaboration available to accomplish greater good in the world.

Beyond Delegating: Inclusive Process Development

When you hire expert consultants, they can help you design the process itself rather than you "assigning" to them.

Even as "delegation-level" VAs develop more expertise, they can take on more responsibility to be involved in the design of the process and certainly in documenting it.

Collaboration or Implementation

For some tasks, you are simply delegating implementation to your VA. You just want them to get it done for you.

Other sorts of tasks require collaboration. For example, developing a website for a new client might involve a graphic designer, code developer, SEO specialist, and InfusionSoft expert working together to design and implement (and adapt) the final product. This requires a much higher level of communication and responsiveness within the team.

When you work in a collaborative environment, with a lot of back-and-forth brainstorming, you need a team communication and tracking tool such as Asana or Teamwork. You also need to have the commitment from everyone to stay on top of the communications within the tool as well as regular information streams.

Between the two ends of the spectrum fall projects such as co-developing a retreat with a partner. You want to share ideas for this one instance, but it's probably not a repeating or ongoing interaction level with that person. For this intermediate level, consider a shared folder through Google Drive or DropBox.

Strategic Alliances and Affiliates

When your collaboration is exclusive to the marketing side, you may be receiving commissions for recommending someone else's product or service, or vice versa. You are not working together on development or delivery.

You may be able to do this on a small scale through warm referrals. An affiliate can refer someone to work with you by sending an e-mail to both you and the potential client introducing you. If the prospect becomes a client, you pay the referrer a commission. (Even if you don't have a formalized arrangement, you should always thank someone who sends you a referral!)

For larger-scale affiliate programs, you'll want internet lead tracking software that notes who sent the lead, when the lead becomes a client, and automates payment of the affiliate on a regular basis. Infusionsoft and Ontraport are the high-end of these tracking packages. You may be able to begin with something simpler, such as Awebber. In either case, hiring this out to a technical expert is highly advisable.

To make it super easy for busy business owners to send you referrals, you will want to provide them with e-mail copy to send out and social media copy to post.

Building an Activated Community

Creating a movement or engaging a tribe illustrates the Conscious Capitalism philosophy of providing multiple forms of value for stakeholders. Not only are your people receiving information from you, they are inspired by and aligned with their peers ... your other clients!

The most common community platform is a Facebook group.

Other tools to consider for hosting course recordings, mastermind forums, etc., include Kajabi, CustomerHub, Member Mouse, and Simplero.

To have an activated community, the tool is the least important element. You must be able to generate discussions, engage your people in conversation, and build relationships for this to be effective.

Joint Development

Usually the term "joint development" refers to co-creating content or an experience with another business. Both businesses market the result and share proceeds. You'll want to be sure to have clear agreements in place about who is responsible for which elements, how proceeds are shared, how risk is shared, and who has rights to the intellectual property going forward.

Tools usually fall into the "collaboration" category discussed previously.

Strategic Philanthropy

Sometimes your business model has you working directly with the cause that moves you most. You could actually be on-site, building wells in Africa.

Other times, you can support your cause openly and transparently through your business by dedicating a portion of proceeds to someone who does the on-the-ground work. Be clear about whether you're donating based on gross sales or profit and walk your talk.

Often you can find other entrepreneurs passionate about the same cause and create a collaboration together to raise awareness and engagement, as well as raising funds. Consider something like wanting to improve children's literacy. You could team up with a small publisher and invite other entrepreneurs to provide chapters. When everyone sells the book, the marketing describes issues in children's literacy. More audiences learn about the issue, businesses who care, and proceeds go to organizations that specialize in solutions.

In Gratitude

My deepest appreciation to you, today's entrepreneur! Your innovative way of tuning in to what's emerging rather than following anyone's label or prescription is precisely what this world needs. We are the ones who birth the next evolution in the realm of commerce, making a better life possible for those who follow behind us.

Because the more we help each other on this conscious entrepreneurial journey, the more difference we can make together, I would be so grateful if you would take a couple minutes and share what you learned from this book in an honest review on our Amazon sales page.

About the Author

Karen Fritz is both an inspirational speaker and transformational educator. She knows that all training is motivational training, and she empowers you with experiential activities for confidence in achieving pragmatic results.

Endlessly fascinated with what makes people tick, Karen has a degree in neuropsychology from the University of Michigan and certifications in Integral Coaching, Divine Navigation, and Awakening Coaching, and has experienced many sacred sites around the globe. She specializes in how people learn—and unlearn—to become more effective in creating the change they wish to see in the world.

In addition to managing software development projects, Karen attended Stanford University to study business, finance, and marketing (no degree). Having found corporate norms too constraining, Karen discovered her own way in the entrepreneurial world. Through her own experiences she has discerned the theoretical from the useful, saving you the time and money of research and repeat mistakes.

As the creator of Purposetivity and the Purpose Driven Process programs, Karen is your creative partner supporting you in both the inner and outer worlds. When she combines her unique abilities to spot patterns in chaos and to communicate visually, her clarity, humor, and liveliness propel participants to transcend outmoded habits and enjoy more fulfillment as they express their purpose.

It would be her joy to guide you to streamline the processes and tools that integrate your professional-personal lifestyle so that everything flows from your purpose and supports you in achieving meaningful contribution for yourself, your tribe, and the world, while flourishing financially and evolving personally.

Let's continue the conversation in the manner that suits you best.

Connect with the Author

karen@PurposeDrivenProcess.com

www.facebook.com/fritz.karen

www.linkedin.com/in/karenfritz

www.PurposeDrivenProcess.com

References

Allen, David. *Getting Things Done: The Art of Stress-free Productivity*. New York: Viking, 2001.

Ardagh, Arjuna. *The Translucent Revolution: How People Just like You Are Waking up and Changing the World*. Novato, CA: New World Library, 2005.

Bach, David. *Smart Couples Finish Rich: 9 Steps to Creating a Rich Future for You and Your Partner*. New York: Broadway, 2001.

Barrett, Richard. *The Values-driven Organization Unleashing Human Potential for Performance and Profit*. Place of Publication Not Identified: Gabler, 2016.

Bono, Edward De. *Lateral Thinking: Creativity Step by Step*. New York: Harper & Row, 1970.

Cameron, Julia. *The Artist's Way: A Spiritual Path to Higher Creativity*. Los Angeles, CA: Jeremy P. Tarcher/Perigee, 1992.

Campbell, Joseph. *The Hero with a Thousand Faces*. Princeton, NJ: Princeton UP, 1972.

Cashman, Kevin, and Jack Forem. *Awakening the Leader Within: A Story of Transformation*. Hoboken, NJ: J. Wiley, 2003.

Childre, Doc Lew, Howard Martin, and Donna Beech. *The HeartMath Solution*. San Francisco, CA: HarperSanFrancisco, 1999.

Csikszentmihaly, Mihaly. *Finding Flow: The Psychology of Engagement with Everyday Life*. 1997

Gardner, Howard. *Intelligence Reframed: Multiple Intelligences for the 21st Century*. New York, NY: Basic, 1999.

Gerber, Michael E. *The E-myth Revisited: Why Most Small Businesses Don't Work and What to Do about It*. New York, NY: HarperBusiness, 2001.

Honeyman, Ryan. *The B Corp Handbook: How to Use Business as a Force for Good*. San Francisco: Berrett-Koehler. 2014.

Katie, Byron, and Stephen Mitchell. *Loving What Is: Four Questions That Can Change Your Life*. New York: Harmony, 2002.

Kiyosaki, Robert T., and Sharon L. Lechter. *Rich Dad, Poor Dad: What the Rich Teach Their Kids about Money— That the Poor and Middle Class Do Not!* Print.

Kornfield, Jack. *After the Ecstasy, the Laundry: How the Heart Grows Wise on the Spiritual Path*. New York: Bantam, 2000.

LaPorte, Danielle. *The Desire Map: A Guide to Creating Goals with Soul*.

Lobenstine, Margaret. *The Renaissance Soul: Life Design for People with Too Many Passions to Pick Just One*. New York: Broadway, 2006.

Mackey, John, and Rajendra Sisodia. *Conscious Capitalism: Liberating the Heroic Spirit of Business*. Boston, MA: Harvard Business Review Press, 2013

Maitri, Sandra. *The Spiritual Dimension of the Enneagram: Nine Faces of the Soul*. New York: Jeremy P. Tarcher/Putnam, 2000.

Maslow, Abraham. *Toward a Psychology of Being*. New York: Wiley, 1998.

McKay, Matthew, Martha Davis, and Patrick Fanning. *Thoughts and Feelings: Taking Control of Your Moods and Your Life*. Oakland, Ca.: New Harbinger Publications, 1997.

Oech, Roger Von. *A Whack on the Side of the Head: How to Unlock Your Mind for Innovation*. New York, NY: Warner, 1983.

Osterwalder, Alexander, Yves Pigneur, Tim Clark, and Alan Smith. *Business Model Generation: A Handbook for Visionaries, Game Changers, and Challengers*. 2010.

Packard, David, David Kirby, and Karen R. Lewis. *The HP Way: How Bill Hewlett and I Built Our Company*. New York: HarperBusiness, 1995.

Renee, Ronda. *Divine Navigation*, www.DivineNavigation.com. Web

Riso, Don Richard., and Russ Hudson. *The Wisdom of the Enneagram: The Complete Guide to Psychological and Spiritual Growth for the Nine Personality Types*. New York: Bantam, 1999.

Sher, Barbara. *Refuse to Choose!: A Revolutionary Program for Doing Everything That You Love*. Emmaus, PA: Rodale, 2007.

Susanka, Sarah. *The Not so Big Life: Making Room for What Really Matters*. New York: Random House, 2007.

Tan, Chade-Meng. *Search inside Yourself: The Unexpected Path to Achieving Success, Happiness (and World Peace)*. New York: HarperOne, 2012.

Twist, Lynne, and Teresa Barker. *The Soul of Money: Reclaiming the Wealth of Our Inner Resources*. New York: W.W. Norton, 2006.

Wilber, Ken. *Integral Psychology: Consciousness, Spirit, Psychology, Therapy*. Boston: Shambhala, 2000.

Willard, Bob. *The Sustainability Advantage: Seven Business Case Benefits of a Triple Bottom Line*. Gabriola Island, B.C.: New Society, 2002.

www.ingramcontent.com/pod-product-compliance
Lightning Source LLC
Chambersburg PA
CBHW060546200326
41521CB00007B/508